God and the Gods

GOD
and
the
Gods

A Compelling Investigation and Personal
Quest for the Truth about God of the
Bible and the Gods of Ancient History

John Greco

iUniverse, Inc.
Bloomington

GOD AND THE GODS
A COMPELLING INVESTIGATION AND PERSONAL
QUEST FOR THE TRUTH ABOUT GOD OF THE BIBLE
AND THE GODS OF ANCIENT HISTORY

Copyright © 2013 John Greco.

All rights reserved. No part of this book may be used or reproduced by any means,
graphic, electronic, or mechanical, including photocopying, recording, taping or by any
information storage retrieval system without the written permission of the publisher
except in the case of brief quotations embodied in critical articles and reviews.

iUniverse books may be ordered through booksellers or by contacting:

iUniverse
1663 Liberty Drive
Bloomington, IN 47403
www.iuniverse.com
1-800-Authors (1-800-288-4677)

Because of the dynamic nature of the Internet, any web addresses or links contained in
this book may have changed since publication and may no longer be valid. The views
expressed in this work are solely those of the author and do not necessarily reflect the
views of the publisher, and the publisher hereby disclaims any responsibility for them.

Any people depicted in stock imagery provided by Thinkstock are models,
and such images are being used for illustrative purposes only.

Certain stock imagery © Thinkstock.

ISBN: 978-1-4759-9596-1 (sc)
ISBN: 978-1-4759-9598-5 (hc)
ISBN: 978-1-4759-9597-8 (e)

Library of Congress Control Number: 2013911432

Printed in the United States of America.

iUniverse rev. date: 6/25/2013

Dedications

This book is dedicated to those who have inspired me to search for the truth and broaden my mind with knowledge.

To my family, who shower me with love and respect.

To my dearest friends Edwin and Kathy Terrana, who show me and my family unselfish happiness by sharing and caring.

To Albert Einstein, who challenged the human mind and made mankind think beyond earthly bounds.

To Nikola Tesla, father of inventions, A/C current, radio waves and the genius that he was.

To Carl Sagan, who saw the Universe in a different light and was right when he said, "Somewhere, something incredible is waiting to be known."

To the Discovery and History channel for the decades that they have provided information and learning documentaries, which broaden the human mind.

To the millions of people who question their existence and purpose on earth.

Special Thanks to:

Jan Sitchin for written permission to use copyright information from her departed husband Zecharia Sitchin, a lifelong pioneer, author, scholar and lecturer devoted to understanding Bible stories and ancient Sumerian text, providing researchers a glimpse into the ancient history of civilization from thousands of clay tablets found in Iraq and preserved for all to see.

Table of Contents

Dedications v

Preface ix

CHAPTER 1   The Story of Modern Man 1

CHAPTER 2   In the Beginning. 27

CHAPTER 3   The Gods of Old 37

CHAPTER 4   Where is Heaven 45

CHAPTER 5   Science Challenges The Bible. 53

CHAPTER 6   One and Only GOD. 69

CHAPTER 7   Show Me the Proof. 95

CHAPTER 8   The Prophets of Old 109

CHAPTER 9   Understanding the Human Soul & Spirit . . . 119

CHAPTER 10   The Puzzle Come's Together 131

CHAPTER 11   Life is a Mystery 141

Recommended Reading 149

References 151

Preface

Understanding what history has preserved in stone and stories we were not told, will forever change the way you think, pray and love. Based on 30 years of research on religion, science, architectural, archeological and astrological facts and finds. Either on purpose or by mistake, the evidence is there and has been for thousands of years. The overwhelming evidence cannot be denied and it is time we humans put the puzzle together. After many years of analysis and conversations with fellow clergymen, I've come to a better understanding concerning the God of the Bible and the Gods of mankind's ancient history. It answered many of my questions. To know the true God, one must first know ancient history. The stories abound and the archeological evidence still stands today. The best way to follow my personal point of view is to know what information has been found and documented. Keep an open mind and decide for yourself based on this information.

Please understand that it is not my intention to change your religion or convert to something new. Just the opposite, I encourage you to follow, believe, worship and share your religious beliefs, no matter what they may be. My purpose is to open your eyes to the possibilities that have accumulated over the years based on the overwhelming evidence and scientific studies of the human body, and the overwhelming evidence of structures and technology human man was incapable of building or engineering alone. The archeological findings made throughout the world today and in the future give credence to the fact that a higher technology had to be involved with our ancient ancestors. The Bible[1] is fact in many ways, but there is more to know. Question everything, including this journal. The truth is out there and most of it is staring us in the face. We just can't seem to tie it together. We as humans, who worship a god we cannot see, need to look in the right places and connect the various pieces of this amazing puzzle together.

Answers are everywhere. The information will make you question the basic teachings from all religions and why stories were not included either on purpose or by mistake. My attempt to dissect and compare the story of human history of Gods from the past[2] and God in the Bible has not been an easy task. It has taken years of research and the relationship between various religions of the world and understanding ancient stories, combining the past with the present, for a clearer understanding of who God was in ancient times and who God of the Bible is. The evolution of human history is an intricate part of who we are. Knowing where we were, will assist us to where we are going. Examining the stories of the Bible and ancient texts found around the world led me to observe the similarities in both. Dissecting them further pointed to various interpretations used to describe something for the first time and how describing something new changed over time based on knowledge and vocabulary. Our elders of time where not capable of calling a flying object what we would call it today. They called it a chariot, metal bird, winged disc or something similar, based on their understanding of what they saw. What would we call something from the future? Would future humans understand what we were trying to explain? Throughout the earth, there are depictions

---

1   King James Bible

2   Sumerian clay tablets

of items that look like advanced technology, yet science dismisses it or overlooks it on purpose.

There are many things science cannot explain such as, what was manna in the Bible? How did they build megalithic structures around the world? I do not know of any other attempt to try and combine the stories of the Bible and the Gods of ancient together. However, this is my personal analysis and interpretation of information that seems eerily familiar and why they may be the same story told in different ways.

WITH THAT SAID, A LITTLE ABOUT ME.

As a young boy, I did what I was told and believed what I was told was true. My parents were Italian Catholics. I, my brothers and sister went to church on Sunday, did not eat meat on Friday and had pasta every Sunday. Growing up in Brooklyn, N.Y., I was expected to become an altar boy in the Catholic Church and go to a Catholic school. Lucky for me, they were right around the corner. In those days the mass was done in Latin, so I had to learn this old language. I collected the money in the money basket and cleaned up the church after mass was done. Every Saturday I would go to confession, recite my sins and do penance. A few Hail Mary's, some Our Fathers and I was done. God and the priest forgave me of any and all my sins. Great, I could do whatever I wanted and as long as I went to confession, I could do it again. After all, the priests were empowered by God himself, so they could forgive sins and other rituals in the name of God and the Catholic Church, right?

I had more time than most for a one- on-one with Father Berrita and other priests. As an inquisitive kid, I asked many questions about the Bible and the statues in the church. By the time I was twelve, I was already asking questions regarding God himself.

The older I got, the more confused I got about God, saints, statues in the church and all religious teachings. I think I asked every possible question to the priests and always got diffrent answers. I did not know it then, but as I got older, some things just made no sense to me and became more confusing. At the age of fifteen, I started reading books from the local library. The more I learned, the more questions I had about religion. You will find in the chapters below my questions were many and the answers were few. It seems the more I read, the more complicated it got. Why was the Bible so hard to read and understand? It was confusing and it seemed stories were missing as they abruptly ended and went on to something else.

My first questions were: Who is God? Where is he? What is God?

All the priest could tell me is what was in the Bible, which was not written by God but others many years later and they did not know God personally.

So many questions went unanswered and I had only more questions as the years went on. I asked priests, clergy, nuns, rabbis, ministers and anyone who would listen or was able to give me some answer I could understand and believe. By the time I was twenty, even more questions arose. Was God a person or a spirit? How could he see everyone at the same time? What was heaven like? Where is heaven? If we were made in his image, does he look human and breathe air? Those were just a few of the questions no one could answer.

I wanted to know the truth and it was not coming from the Bible. I decided to go on my own to see how other religions worshiped and how their stories were told. It was not until the internet came to be and I was in my late twenties that I was able to research more about the many questions I had about God and the Bible. The internet was relatively new at the time and information was very limited. In my mid-thirties, I became a minister of the Universal Church, which is a church of no special denomination. We preach of God in many religious forms. You could call it a Universal Church of a Universal God. I have had many one–on-one conversations with world religion representatives and studied the relationship between archeology and architectural findings around the world. The more I started to see the intricate and complex designs, the more I realized there is more to this than meets the eye. Early man could not have made these fascinating structures without knowing complex mathematics and architectural design. History tells us primitive men were simple hunter gatherers and made simple tools. However, this cannot be true.

They built temples of worship that exceed modern construction today and were not as dumb as we are led to believe. They had to possess knowledge and understanding that must have been lost or forgotten over time. I began a personal quest to find the connection between our ancient ancestors and their stories of the Gods who lived among them and may have been involved with the construction of these megalithic structures built around the world. Every day more information appears and more findings are unearthing that seem to point to a past we are unable to comprehend because pieces of the puzzle of life are missing. My personal quest to solve the puzzle of life will perhaps go on forever. Our history of mankind may not be what we have read or been taught. Or it could have been a deliberate attempt to hide the truth about the origins of man, for some unknown reason.

After 30 years of research and conversations, I came to an understanding that made more sense to me and answered many questions I had. Of course, this is only my opinion and to me, a more acceptable or plausible answer based on the information uncovered through the research by many others and myself.

Come with me on a journey and uncover a miniscule piece of information not covered in national news and secretly hidden from the public for reasons unknown. Volumes of additional information that could fill a library room with stories and artifacts off limits to mankind. This manuscript touches merely a few of the many secrets society is hiding for their own benefit. They are small pieces of a multidimensional puzzle in unraveling the real origin of mankind and why it would change our history of who we are and where we came from.

CHAPTER 1

The Story of Modern Man

Genesis tells us that God made man and woman, and yet, Genesis also says that Adam was alone, so God made Eve from his rib while he slept. Adam was made with a mate in Genesis 1:27. What happened to the first woman, if God made Eve later in Genesis 2:17? Why does the Bible not explain more clearly who the first woman was?

For those who are not familiar with Genesis, here is the relevant scripture.

> So God created mankind in his own image, in the image of God he created them; male and female he created them. (Genesis 1:27, KJV)

> But for Adam no suitable helper was found. So the Lord God caused the man to fall into a deep sleep and while he was sleeping, he took one of the man's ribs and then closed up the place with flesh. Then the Lord God made a woman from the rib he had taken out of the man and he brought her to the man. The man said, "This is now bone of my bones and flesh of my flesh; she shall be called 'woman,' for she was taken out of man." (Genesis 2:19, KJV)

This is the beginning of the Bible, and already we have a problem with the creation story. Did the writers of the Christian Bible forget something here? The Bible does not mention who the first woman, whose name was Lilith, until later. Genesis, of course, mentions Adam and Eve, but it does not mention Lilith as the first mate by name. However, the Bible does make reference to her in a later chapter. Lilith is included in the writings of the Torah, and the Christian Bible used the Torah as its source of information. Why did the writers of the Bible leave out Lilith? Lilith is worshiped by a secret society and hidden from the public even today.

Every July, some of the richest and most powerful men in the world gather at a campground in Monte Rio, Calif., for two weeks of heavy drinking, super-secret talks and druid worship, a group of elites, including some past presidents join at a secret Bohemian Grove Club meeting. The waiting list is thirty-three years long, and the grove has several hundred members.

From what I understand about this secret society, they participate in a ritual worshipping of kings or gods of ancient history. This ritual includes human sacrifice; of course the sacrifice is a mock burning. Nevertheless, it is a worship and ritual as old as time, and these powerful leaders enjoy every minute of the parties that follow. The members are not allowed to discuss business deals. The only exception was in 1942, with the planning of the Manhattan Project, which led to the creation of the atom bomb. The club is very private and heavily guarded, so little is known as to what transactions really take place. In 2000, Texas-based filmmaker Alex Jones infiltrated the group.[3] Jones entered the camp with a hidden camera and was able to film a Grove ceremony, which took place on stage one night. During the ceremony, members wore costumes and cremated a coffin effigy called "Care" before a forty-foot-tall owl. The representation of

---

3 Alex Jones is a producer, writer, commentator, and investigator. www.infowars. com

this owl figure is supposedly an ancient god or king called Moloch.[4] Moloch was a god worshipped by the Phoenicians and Canaanites. Moloch had associations with a particular kind of propitiatory child sacrifice by parents. Moloch appears in the book of Deuteronomy and in the book of Leviticus. At this ritual, officials speak about information not privy to the public. The group calls them private interest talks.

How odd that they would worship old gods and have an owl in this ritual. Even stranger is the fact that this ancient ritual is still happening today. This ritual may date back to the creation of Adam and the place where Lilith resided after leaving Adam.[5] The Jewish Midrashim on Proverbs states that Lilith was created expressly to harm or kill newborn infants. In fact, SIDS (sudden infant death syndrome) was associated with Lilith. However, Lilith swore that she would not harm any infant wearing an amulet with the images and or names of the three angels on it. Is there a connection between Moloch and Lilith pertaining to children? The cremation effigy at this private meeting is that of a child.

In the Jewish Torah, Lilith was Adam's first wife and was created at the same time and from the same earth as Adam

A possible explanation for Lilith in the Bible may be found in Isaiah 34:12.

> "Her nobles shall be no more, nor shall kings be proclaimed there; all her princes are gone. Her castles shall be overgrown with thorns, her fortresses with thistles and briers. She shall become an abode for jackals and a haunt for ostriches. Wildcats shall meet with desert beasts, satyrs shall call to

---

4   "Do not give any of your children to be sacrificed to Moloch, for you must not profane the name of your God. I am the LORD" (Leviticus 18:21).

5   Jewish folklore.

one another; There shall the Lilith repose and find for herself a place to rest. There the hoot owl shall nest and lay eggs, hatch them out and gather them in her shadow."

This is the only mention of Lilith in the Bible. The Bible can be perplexing. The writers selected what went in and what stayed out. Was there a reason for that? Did the Catholic Church purposely leave out this other woman?

For thousands of years, man has given homage to a God. The Muslims, Jews, Christians, and other religions pray to one God. Hundreds of thousands of scholars since the beginning of time itself have asked who or what is God?

Jews say God is the father of all mankind, while Christians say God is the Supreme Being, just God; he is the alpha and the omega. Muslims believe that God is the all-powerful Creator of a perfect, ordered universe. God has many names from the different religious sects.

- Some of the ninety-nine Muslim names of God (*Asma al-Husna*) in the Qur'an are the Creator, the Fashioner, the Life-Giver, the Provider, the Opener, the Bestower, the Prevailer, the Reckoner, the Recorder, the King of Kingship, and the Lord of the Worlds.

- Some of the Jewish names of God are Yahweh, Jehovah, Elohim (God or Authority), El (Mighty One), Shaddai (Almighty), Adonai (Master), Elyon (Most High), and Avinu (Our Father).

- The Christians have the fewest number of names for God. They are Almighty, Lord, Messiah, Alpha and the Omega, and Father.

- Some may laugh at the notion that the word *God* has any origin or association with Hindu Sanskrit, but there is proof that the word *God* may have been used by the Assyrians in 2400 BC to 612 BC.

The Sumerians believed their God was Elohim, meaning "those that came from above," also known as Anu, Assur, or Ashur, leader of the Annunaki. The Sumerians' writings are documented as the oldest known to man, older than the Bible and the Torah by thousands of years. It is believed that the writers of the Torah and Bible used Assyrian writings as the basis for creation and the flood, as in the story of Gilgamesh. In fact, there are some seven thousand references to a great flood on earth in the past from around the world.

Thousands of clay tablets[6] written by the Sumerians were found in Iraq. Dr. Zechariah Sitchin interpreted these tablets over a thirty-year period, telling an astonishing story of how mankind came to be.

So who were the Assyrians and Sumerians?

According to the cuneiform Sumerian tablets found in Iraq, Mr. Sitchin interpreted their story.

Between 4500 and 2400 B.C., complex societies appeared in the form of cities and fortifications, with specialization in building and writing. These features were associated with the Sumerians and they quickly spread to other parts of Mesopotamia, including Assyria. In Assyria, settlements had become large and were guarded by fortified walls, which would imply the risk of attack from outside foes, hence the need for defense and warfare. It is in Assyria where the mythological foundation of the Old Testament is found. It is here that the story of the flood originates, 2000 years before the Old Testament is written. It is here that the first epic is written, the Epic

---

6   Cuneiform documents were written on clay tablets by means of a blunt reed for a stylus.

of Gilgamesh, with its universal and timeless theme of the struggle and purpose of humanity. It is here that civilization itself is developed and handed down to future generations. Here where the first steps in the unification of the Middle East were taken. By bringing under Assyrian rule the diverse groups in the area from Iran to Egypt. They broke down barriers and prepared the way for the cultural unification which facilitated a great nation in the Middle East. The writings talk about a non-human called the Anunnaki. They supposedly live on a planet called Nibiru, which in the past was in our solar system. This may be the lost planet that is now called planet X. According to the text, The Anunnaki were in need of gold and found it on planet earth. The leaders along with council, decided to make man from the primitive life forms already here on earth. At the time the monkey, or what we call Homo erectus was the closest to human they could find. Over time and many attempts, they decided to engineer the genes of themselves and this monkey life form to create a new man, which we call Homo sapiens. Sound familiar? Adam and Eve? Could this be the creation mentioned in the Bible? Was Adam genetically engineered to be a man on earth? Remember these writings were written some 2000 years before the Torah and the Bibles Old Testament.

CUNEIFORM CLAY TABLETS

Cuneiform script is one of the earliest known systems of writing. Emerging in Sumer in the late 4th millennium BC (the Uruk IV period), cuneiform writing began as a system of pictographs. In the third millennium, the pictorial representations became simplified and more abstract as the number of characters in use grew smaller, from about 1000 in the Early Bronze Age to about 400 in late Bronze Age (Hittite cuneiform).

The original Sumerian script was adapted for the writing of the Akkadian, Eblaite, Elamite, Hittite, Luwian, Hattic, Hurrian and

Urartian languages and it inspired the Ugaritic and old Persian alphabets. Cuneiform writing was gradually replaced by the Phoenician alphabet during the Neo-Assyrian Empire and by the 2nd century AD, the script had become extinct. All knowledge of how to read it was forgotten until it began to be deciphered in the 19th century. Cuneiform documents were written on clay tablets by means of a blunt reed for a stylus. The impressions left by the stylus were wedge shaped, thus giving rise to the name cuneiform "wedge shaped", from the Latin cuneus "wedge".

The cuneiform writing system was in use for more than 22 centuries, through several stages of development, from the 34th century BC down to the 2nd century AD.[3] It was completely replaced by alphabetic writing (in the general sense) in the course of the Roman era, and there are no Cuneiform systems in current use. For this reason, it had to be deciphered from scratch in the 19th century Certain signs to indicate names of gods, countries, cities, vessels, birds, trees, etc., are known as determinants and were the Sumerian signs for the terms in question, added as a guide for the reader. Proper names continued to be usually written in purely "logographic" fashion.

Assyrian cuneiform method of writing continued through the end of the Babylonian and Assyrian empires, although there were periods when "purism" was in fashion and there was a marked tendency to spell out the words laboriously in preference to using signs with a phonetic complement. Yet even in those days, the Babylonian syllabary remained a mixture of logographic and phonemic writing.

APE-MAN

Let's look at what history has to say about the theory of monkey to man. I will list the finds and the order that they were found. Before I continue, answer this question. "If God made man (Adam and Eve), then who or what were Neanderthal man, Australopithecus Afaronsis, Taung child, Homo Habilis, Hominids and Homo Erectus?" We do know that Homo sapiens are considered to be modern man, but who or what are the others before modern man.? In a biblical question, did God make all these other ape-like creatures before he made man? Records do show these other man-like creatures were much older than Homo sapiens. According to the recent African ancestry theory, [7] modern humans evolved in Africa possibly from Homo heidelbergensis and migrated out of the continent some 50,000 to 100,000 years ago, replacing local populations of Homo erectus and Homo Neanderthal. The human species developed a much larger brain than that of other primates – typically 1,330 (cc) in modern humans, over twice the size of that of a chimpanzee or gorilla. A number of other changes have also characterized the evolution of humans. Among them are increased importance on vision rather than smell, a smaller gut, loss of body hair, evolution of sweat glands, a change in the shape of the dental arcade from being u-shaped to being parabolic, development of a chin (only found in Homo sapiens). The closest living relatives of humans are gorillas (genus Gorilla) and chimpanzees (Genus Pan). With the sequencing of both the human and chimpanzee genome, current estimates of the similarity between their DNA sequences range between 95% and 99%. By comparing mitochondrial DNA which is inherited only from the mother, geneticists have concluded that the last female common ancestor whose genetic marker is found in all modern humans, the so-called mitochondrial Eve, must have lived around 200,000 years ago. The question of the relation between these early fossil species and the hominid lineage is still to be resolved

- In 1856 in Germany, workers were digging for limestone in a cave. What they found was a skull cap of what was

---

7 Mitochondrial Eve refers to the matrilineal most recent common ancestor (MRCA) of modern humans

called Neanderthal man. It had large eye sockets and an uncommonly large nasal cavity and was dated to be 40,000 years old. Since then, over 300 were found in Europe.

- It appears that Neanderthal man coexisted with Homo erectus which came from Africa and the Middle East. These two are the earliest of man. There are skulls that are much older. A recent study by the Genome Research Institute found that Homo Sapian and Neanderthal man were not the same at all. Confirmed by DNA testing, they were entirely different species.

- Homo erectus was found in Africa and dated to be 800,000 years old. He walked upright and was six feet tall with a brain cavity two-thirds the size of modern man.

- Homo Habilis man (tool Maker) was dated to be 1.75 million years old found in South Africa.

- Taung Child was dated to be two million years old and was about three feet tall, found in South Africa in 1960.

- The oldest skull along with 50 pieces of bone, were found by Donald Yohanson and others in Ethiopia near an old lake bed. Making the news in recent times, she was called Lucy and dated to be 3.2 million years old.

- Other skulls were found in Java in 1891 dated to be one half to one million years old. It's odd to have factual proof that there were other ape-man like creatures living on earth as long as 3.5 million years ago.

According to writer Zecharia Sitchin,[8]ancient Sumerian clay tablets

---

8   Zecharia Sitchin- Author of "The Cosmic Code" collection of 12 book series.

reveal that gods from another planet Nibiru, which orbits our Sun every 3,600 years arrived on Earth some 450,000 years ago and around 200,000 years ago, created humans by genetic engineering of female monkeys. As we see from above, ape-man like creatures did live on earth before the gods from another planet came to earth. Is it possible these gods used DNA or genes from this early ape-man to genetically engineer modern man (Homo sapiens) mixing their DNA with ape-monkey to create a hybrid man? Were these gods the same God of the Bible, or are they different gods? If you read the above, than the timing would be correct as Neanderthal and Homo erectus lived 400,000 – 200,000 years ago and coexisted, but were different according to DNA testing.

According to some scientists, there is no significant explanation for human beings to be on this planet. Their reasoning is, evolution has not changed over extended time concerning primates and apes in matters of brain functions. If humans were genetically the same as primates, we would not have developed as fast as we have as far as brain function. Without a significant change in human DNA at some time in the past, we would never have developed to be who we are today. We humans are the only species on earth who are capable of speech. What stops apes and monkeys and all other species on earth from speech is a genetic marker.

- Scientists have identified the Fox –P2 gene in human DNA, which may be responsible for speech and we are the only species that have it.

- According to the University of Chicago[9] in a report in 2004 while studying the brain, "It seems that the human brain went through a dramatic genetic change sometime around 50,000 years ago".

---

9   Howard Hughes Medical Institute December 29,2004 News Report

Evolution could not have been responsible for such a drastic change in such a remarkably short time. Someone or something of superior intelligence had to modify hominids DNA for such a change to happen so quickly. The question is, was it God or the Anunnaki gods that changed early ape man into modern man? The problem I have is, if God made man in the beginning, what happened to our brain or DNA some 50,000 years ago according to scientific studies? Are they wrong, or have they found something?

By now you are saying, "What proof is there and how do we know?" The epic story of creation was found on seven clay tablets, the same amount in the creation story in the Bible. The differences is that the Bible said God created everything in seven days, while the Sumerian text say it took many years just to make early man. It said nothing about the creation of the universe or planets, as they were already here. There were and still are over 7000 clay tablets in existence, possibly more. They are considered to be historical evidence of an ancient civilization that lived in the southern region of Iraq. The location where the four rivers meet the Garden of Eden also known as the birthplace of creation. When you read the information everything sounds eerily familiar to what we have learned and are still trying to understand today. I will put it in perspective using the timeline in a later chapter. I decided to put this information in later chapters in an effort to keep the flow of reading easier for the reader.

Working from the same archaeological discoveries, artifacts and recovered records as archaeologists and linguists have for two hundred years. Sitchin propounds – proves in his interpretation and as documented proof from the clay tablet writings, that the Anunnaki (Sumerian translation: "those who came down from the heavens"; Anakeim, Nefilim, Elohim; Egyptian: Neter), an advanced civilization from the tenth planet in our solar system landed in the Persian Gulf area around 432,000 years ago colonized the planet with the purpose of obtaining large quantities of gold for repair of their planet's atmosphere.

Genesis 2:11 tells us that God saw there was gold in the area of Eden, specifically at Pishon, which was one of four rivers flowing through the lower region of Iraq. One must ask why was gold so important to be mentioned in this chapter. Man (Adam) had no need or use for gold. So the question is, why mention the fact that God of the Bible saw there was gold in this area. Was God in need of gold, or as the Sumerian tablet which mentions the need for gold represent a hint of truth based on their tablets. Gold is mentioned 359 times in the King James Bible. One must entertain the idea that the Sumerian tablets mention that the Anunnaki landed in the Sinai region in search of gold, which was in the area, confirmed in the genesis chapter. Apparently, gold was so important it was mentioned in the Genesis chapter of creation, which is the beginning of God's involvement on earth. Adam had no need for gold and it had no value of which to trade for.

Some 250,000 years ago, the recovered Sumerian documents tell us, their lower echelon miners rebelled against the conditions in the mines and the Anunnaki directorate decided to create a creature to take their place. Enki, their chief scientists and Ninhursag their chief medical officer, after getting no satisfactory results splicing animal and Homo erectus genes (AKA Greek myth demigods) merged their Anunnaki genes with that of Homo erectus and produced us.

The genetically engineered Homo sapiens were a genetically bicameral species made for the purpose of mining. Because we were a hybrid, we could not procreate. An example of this is a cross between a tiger and a lion, called a Liger. The offspring was always male and they grew to five times the size and weight of the parent. They were also sterile, meaning they could not reproduce. Science is still trying to create a sterile male today. The demand for us as workers became greater and we were genetically manipulated to reproduce. Eventually we became so numerous that some left from the Anunnaki city centers, gradually spreading over the planet. Having become a stable genetic stock and developing more precociously than, perhaps, the Anunnaki had anticipated, the Anunnaki began to be attracted to human females as sexual partners and fathered children in the Bible account. Giants were born of these unions. As stated above, the male liger was much larger and weighed four times as much as the parents because of a genetic mutation which caused both giants and ligers to grow to enormous sizes. Check the internet for giant skeletons and ligers. You will find tons of info, pictures and videos. According to scientists, everyone can be traced back to one woman from Africa genetically.

Read Genesis: 6 which record's the interaction of sons of God and daughters of man. For the Anunnaki leaders,(gods) this was unacceptable to the majority, the Anunnaki high council decided to wipe out the human population through a flood that was predictable when Nibiru, the tenth planet in our solar system and the Anunnaki home planet came through our solar system again on one of it's periodic 3600 year returns. Its next pass is calculated to be the year 2087. Some humans were saved (Noah and his family) by the action of the Anunnaki official Enki, who was sympathetic to the humans he had originally genetically created. For thousands of years, we were their slaves, their workers, their servants and their soldiers in their political battles among themselves. The Anunnaki used us in the construction of their palaces, temples, cities, mining refining complexes and their astronomical installations on all continents providing their superior knowledge and using the massive amount of Homo sapiens. They expanded from Mesopotamia to Egypt to India to South and Central America and the stamp of their presence can be found in the farthest reaches of the planet.

Around 6000 years ago they, realizing they were going to phase off the planet after their mining operations would end, began gradually to bring humans to independence. Sumer, a human civilization, startling in its "sudden", mature and highly advanced character, was set up under their tutelage in Mesopotamia. Human kings were inaugurated as go-between foremen of the human populations answering to the Anunnaki. A strain of humans genetically enhanced with more Anunnaki genes. A bloodline of rulers in a tradition of servants of the people, were initiated (rulers or watchers). These designated humans were taught technology, mathematics, astronomy, advanced crafts and the ways of the advanced Anunnaki. Rulers were taught that there existed a robust highly possessed tradition of preserving the bloodline known as Blue Bloods, which should be kept within the family of rulers or watchers. This may be the reason almost all Egyptian rulers married within family members.

Another interesting fact is the description of Jacob's ladder which appears in Genesis 28:10-19. Jacob came to a place and stayed there that night because the sun had set. Taking one of the stones of the place he put it under his head and lay down in that place to sleep. He dreamed and behold, there was a ladder set up on the earth and the top of it reached to heaven; and behold, the angels of God were ascending and descending on it. It is also known as Jacob's Pillow Stone and the Tanist Stone. Its size is about 26 inches (660 mm) by 16.75 inches (425 mm) by 10.5 inches (270 mm) and its weight is approximately 336 pounds (152 kg). The top bears chisel marks. The Stone of Destiny was last used in 1953 for the formal ceremony of Queen Elizabeth II. The Stone of Scone, also known as the Stone of Destiny and often referred to in England as The Coronation Stone is an oblong block of red sandstone used for centuries in the coronation of the monarchs of Scotland and later the monarchs of England, Great Britain and the United Kingdom. The connection to blue blood is the fact that this stone, staff and crown represented hierarchies passed down from the first known king in history in Sumer and is practiced in many monarchy rituals to present day. The hall of records in Egypt shows the items used, such as the staff of rule, the headdress of kingship and the authority of the ruler.

Every Record of civilization around the world has recorded a God or gods creating mankind and coexisting with them on earth. In fact, that was the birth of the religious revolution for all cultures. They worship and deify their particular God or gods. All religions are the same with the exception of whom or what they worship. The Anunnaki had a god and they also had demigods. Most religions are structured the same way with God, demigods, leaders and servants.

Father Jose Funes,[10] a Jesuit astronomer, director of the Vatican Observatory suggested in an interview that the possibility of "brother extraterrestrials" poses no problem for Catholic theology. "a multiplicity of creatures exists on Earth, so there could be other beings, also intelligent, created by God," Funes explained. "This does not conflict with our faith because we cannot put limits on the creative freedom of God."

From the above chapter, we see the possibilities of Greek mythology, mankind made in his image and the structuring of hierarchy such as kings and leaders of their time. We can also see the correlation between the creation of mankind from both the Bible and the Sumerian tablets. They are the same story told in two different ways. The Bible is brief, whereas the Sumerian text is expanded. They both created man and the similarities of seven days and seven tablets parallel each other extremely closely. Is it possible creation was by an Anunnaki god, Enki? Keep in mind; no one knows who God of the Bible really is, and Judgment is up to you.

THE EVIDENCE SUPPORTS THE SITCHIN THEORY

Most solar systems have a companion sun within their structure. Either it is a red dwarf or a brown dwarf star. The question becomes, why does our Sun not have a companion star too? Recent discoveries have confirmed that our Sun may have a companion star, which is in

---

10   Vatican City, May 13, 2008 / 01:59 pm (CNA).- The Director of the Vatican's Observatory

an elliptical orbit. However, it cannot be confirmed it belongs to our solar system. According to 6000- year-old scrolls with depictions on them which were made by the Sumerians, tell us our solar system had ten planets within it. It also named the planets using different names than we call them now. They also tell of structures on Mars used as a way station for the Anunnaki and water existed on the surface. Stretched out at a distance of 205 to 300 million miles from the Sun, is a band of asteroids known as the asteroid belt. Sumerian text and NASA say that the asteroid belt is called the hammered bracelet (which is also in the Bible), and was once a part of the earth before a great collision with Nibiru.

The odd thing is, no one knew the earth was round and yet the picture is worth a thousand words and the proof is in the Sumerian pictogram which shows all our solar system, including a planet which was called Nibiru. NASA has been on the hunt for this planet for over 30 years and I think if they find it, the question has to be, will they tell us? I predict that NASA is looking for structures on Mars with the new rover recently sent. Will they tell us what they actually find? Several years ago a probe sent back pictures from Mars showing some sort of pyramid structure and the famous face of Cydonia. NASA claimed this was a light refraction and that was the end of it. I wonder what else is there? I look at it this way, if major discoveries of structures on Mars are made public, it would rewrite history and destroy religion as we know it all with one blow. The question then becomes, could we and are we ready to learn our true past history? The only real proof will have to come from an outside source other than NASA which is government controlled. Because of copyrights, I have not included these pictures within this book. However I encourage you to search the Sumerian pictograms both online and in many museums around the world. You too will be scratching your head saying, "Is this possible?" The information on these clay tablets even tells us the colors of these planets and they had no telescopes back in the day. NASA has confirmed the facts that these 6000

—years- old pictogram sand clay tablets of our solar system to be most accurate to date concerning the planet's size, color and the fact that the Sun is in the center. They also confirm that at some time in our past, planet earth was hit by a large planet, some four times the size of earth and sent earth (which back then was called Tiamat) into a different area of our solar system. Earth was once further away from the Sun, suggesting that prior to a grand cataclysm described in the Babylonian Enuma elish, the Earth was the planet which the Sumerians called Tiamat. The planetary impact was in the Pacific Ocean and there is a gorge called Mariana trench, the deepest depth of all the oceans on earth. Every day we hear or see NASA has found a planet within the goldilocks zone and they predict billions more are out there in just our Milky Way system alone. There is a pictorial scroll in the British museum which shows a human on one side and an Anunnaki on the other side with a spaceship in the middle of them. The ironic part is, on the bottom is a fish which represents the age of Pisces which ends in 2100. It also shows Mars as the meeting place. NASA is pushing hard to launch humans to mars and as of 2012 we have sent a new car-size rover to check the surface out with intent to send humans soon. This presents a new question. How is it possible that this pictogram predicts something to happen in our future? I do not know but it is on display in a British Museum.

Examples to giants living on earth are recorded in the Genesis 6 and the Sumerian text. Additional information pertaining to Anunnaki or giants on earth may be supported by some of the many stories listed.

Findings include:

- A team of anthropologists found a mysterious burial in the jungle near the city of Kigali Rwanda (Central Africa). The remains belong to gigantic creatures that bear little resemblance to humans. The creatures were tall approximately seven feet. Their heads were disproportionately large and they had no mouth, nose or eyes.

- In the summer of 1937 a group of Chinese scientists led by Professor Chi Putei surveyed the caves of Mount Bayan-Kara-Ula. Inside they found skeletons with excessively large heads and puny bodies. Professor of Beijing University Zum Umniu deciphered several inscriptions on stone plates and determined the grooved letters narrated that approximately 12 thousand years ago some flying objects crashed in these mountains.

- Not that long ago in one of the ancient Egyptian tombs a mummy of a man 2.5 meters tall was found. It had no nose or ears and its mouth was very wide and had no tongue. According to archaeologist Gaston de Villars, the age of the mummy is approximately 4 thousand years.

- The Bible mentions giants and is very specific to the fact that they lived during the days of old and where men of old. The Sumerians claim the Anunnaki were very tall beings and all their pictorials show this. Goliath was a giant and came from a group of giants from the Middle East. The stories both introduce giants in their scriptures. The giants were between seven to nine feet and were the average size.

- The Nephilim (giants) were on the earth in those days (and also afterward when the sons of God would consort with the daughters of man, who would bear to them). They were the mighty who, from old, were men of devastation. God saw that the wickedness of these giants were great upon the earth and that every product of the thoughts of their heart was but always evil. The Nephilim were presumably destroyed in the flood, but further giants are reported in the Torah, including the Anakites (Numbers 13:28-33), the Emites (Deuteronomy 2:10) and, in Joshua, the Rephaites (Joshua 12:4).

• The Bible also tells of Gog and Magog, who later entered into European folklore and of the famous battle between David and the Philistine giant Goliath.

I cannot help but think of André the giant who was a wrestler in recent times. He was diagnosed with a pituitary gland problem which made his body grow. He eventually died from complications. He stood seven feet, four inches and weighed 475 pounds. His diagnosis was known as gigantism[11], a growth hormone gone crazy. André was one of thousands with this disorder.

From these findings of strange skeletal remains, which were not made very public, one has to question, what these creatures were and where did they come from? They have been found all around the world.

GOVERNMENT OFFICIALS MEET ZECHARIAH SITCHIN AND COMPARE NOTES

A key underpinning of the Sitchin paradigm is the existence, now or in the past, of a tenth planet in our solar system, this was the home planet of the Anunnaki with the size, orbit and characteristics described by Sitchin demonstrated in the Enuma Elish and corroborated by Harrington, former chief of the U.S. Naval Observatory, now deceased.

Tombaugh discovered Pluto in 1930. Christie, of the U.S. Naval Observatory, discovered Charon, Pluto's moon, in 1978. The characteristics of Pluto derivable from the nature of Charon

---

11 Gigantism is usually caused by a tumor on the pituitary gland of the brain. It causes growth of the hands, face, and feet.

demonstrated that there must still be a large planet undiscovered because Pluto could not be the cause of the residuals, the wobbles in the orbital paths of Uranus and Neptune clearly identifiable. The IRAS Infrared Astronomical Satellite during '83 –'84 produced observations of a tenth planet so robust that one of the astronomers on the project said "all that remains is to name it" – from that point, the information has become curiously guarded.

In 1992 Harrington and Van Flandern of the Naval Observatory, working with all the information they had at hand, published their findings and opinion that there is, indeed, a tenth planet, even calling it an "intruder" planet. The search was narrowed to the southern skies, below the ecliptic. Harrington invited Sitchin, having read his book and translations of the Enuma Elish, to a meeting at his office and they correlated the current findings with the ancient records.

The recovered Enuma Elish document, a history of the formation of our solar system and more, says that at the time Mercury, Venus, Mars, Jupiter, Uranus and Saturn were in place, there was a Uranus-sized planet called Tiamat in orbit between Mars and Jupiter. Earth was not in place yet. A large wandering planet called Nibiru was captured into the system gravitationally. As it passed by the outer planets it caused the anomalies of their moons, the tilting of Uranus on its side, the dislodging of Pluto from being a moon of Saturn to its own planetary orbit. Its path was bent by the gravitational pull of the large planets, first its satellites collided with the large planet Tiamat and on a second orbit through Nibiru collided with Tiamat driving the larger part of it into what is now earth's orbit to re congeal as earth, dragging its moon with it to become our moon with all its anomalies. The shattered debris of Tiamat's smaller part became the asteroid belt, comets and meteorites.

The gouge of our Pacific basin is an impressive testimony to a collisional event. Nibiru settled into a 3600 year elliptical retrograde orbit (opposite direction to all the other planets) orbit around our sun, coming in through the asteroid belt region between Mars and Jupiter at perigee and swinging far out past Pluto at apogee. Harrington acknowledged that his information agreed with all these details and maps they each had drawn of the orbits were almost indistinguishable. The current probable location of Nibiru (Planet X, our tenth) estimated by both was the same.

In light of the evidence already obtained through the use of the Pioneer 10 and 11 and two Voyager space craft, the Infrared Imaging Satellite (IRAS, '83-84) and the clear and unequivocal statements of Harrington when consulting with Sitchin, that the search has already been accomplished, in fact that the planet has already been found. As of the present time 2012, not only has this planet been found, it has been named as planet X. NASA is tracking it and is being called a possible twin Sun, a brown star, and of course Nibiru. An internet search will provide thousands of sites with information, as well as YouTube videos.

The ancient records are exceedingly clear. The passage of the tenth planet Nibiru once every 3600 years through the inner solar system affects the earth, sometimes in catastrophic ways. It is particularly a probable cause of pole shifts, pole reversals, changes in the processional movement, perhaps even catastrophic bombardment by asteroid-size space debris that it may drag along with it. Since it passes through the asteroid belt area between Mars and Jupiter and its orbital path may vary depending on the position of the other planets when it comes through, it may have been responsible for the devastation of Mars. The Vatican maintains an astronomical observatory may have access to information that prompts them to make the startling statements as a voice of the Vatican. A statement by the Catholic Church a few years ago stated the possibility of brother extraterrestrials poses no problem for Catholic theology. As a multiplicity of creatures exists on Earth, so there could be other beings, also intelligent, created by

God, This does not conflict with our faith because we cannot put limits on the creative freedom of God.

Purportedly out of place in time are

- Artifacts, megalithic structures, intricate designs in granite, toys, tools, technical devices, depictions and documents which have come to light through archaeological excavation or discovery.

Almost everyone is familiar through published works or documentaries, with the clay pot batteries still containing the electrodes from the Iraqi desert dated 2500 B.C., the flyable model airplane from a pyramid tomb, the sophisticated machining of stone requiring the most advanced techniques we know today, the 1000 –ton precision-cut blocks of stone in a temple foundation that we could not handle, an ancient relief frieze from an Abydos temple depicting rockets, airplanes and even a helicopter, etc. The most recent and quite astonishing is the rediscovery of monatomic gold by David Hudson[12], (Monatomic are superconductors that at room temperature have anti-gravity properties and are only now being investigated by the advanced physics community) Hudson's discovery correlated the suppressed discovery of the Anunnaki gold processing plant on Mt. Horeb by Sir Flinders Petrie in 1889. It demonstrates that the monatomic were already known at least 3000 years ago. These parts coupled with evidence from many disciplines and the historical records from the Sumerian tablets indicate that an advanced civilization existed in those times possessing a high technology and that civilization was indeed the Anunnaki.

Note: In an earlier section, you read about the giants graves found in Africa. They were found near the gold mining facilities mentioned

---

12 Monatomic gold is believed to have been eaten by the ancient Egyptians and was depicted to be a food of the gods which would assist the Egyptians in unlocking their mental and spiritual abilities

in the Sumerian tablets. Could these have been the Anunnaki? They certainly were not human. Archeologists have confirmed the gold mines within the area were approximately 100,000 – 150,000 years old which concludes, someone was mining gold for some apparent reason.

The recorded historical documentation for the existence and deeds of the Anunnaki has become gradually available to us only since the early 1800's. The excavation of the ancient sites of Mesopotamia brought to light the amazingly advanced civilization of Sumer, and with it, thousands of clay tablets containing not only records of commerce, marriages, military actions and advanced astronomical calculation systems, but the history of the Anunnaki themselves. It is clear from those records that the Sumerians knew these aliens to be real flesh and blood living among them. The library of the ruler Ashurbanipal at Nineveh was discovered to have burnt down and the clay tablets held there were fired, preserving them for our reading. One of the most impressive finds very recently has been a sealed nine foot by six foot room in Sipper holding neatly arranged on shelves a set of some 400 elaborate clay tablets containing an unbroken record of the history of those ancient times, including the seven tablets of creation.

Technically, it is six tablets of creation, because the seventh exalts the leaders for their deeds. The Bible has six days and the seventh day of rest. Are these stories the same, just told by different cultures? The evidence is so overwhelming that if it were not for those with the power to suppress it would have been accepted and our world view changed centuries ago or sooner.

The location of the Anunnaki laboratory according to the tablets is where the first humans were literally produced in east central Africa just above their gold mines. This falls precisely on the map where the mitochondrial DNA "search for Eve" places the first woman Homo sapiens and in the same period. Remember in an earlier statement I made above, "We humans can all be traced back to one woman from Africa". This is known as the Eve factor in human DNA research. The gold mining engineers of Africa in the present have found 100,000-year-old gold mines in that area. The evidence of, and description of advanced genetic engineering is all there in the ancient documents. Our rapid progress from inception to going to Mars soon after only 250,000 years does not correspond to the million year periodicities of slow evolutionary development of other species such as Homo erectus or several other species of early man before us. As so, many thinkers have pointed out we are radically and unusually different than any creature on earth, including monkeys and apes.

How could the Anunnaki, clearly described as comfortable in earth's gravity and atmosphere and very similar to current humans in all ways, have evolved on a planet within our solar system whose orbital apogee takes it into the deep cold of space for much of its orbit? The ancient records repeatedly describe Nibiru as a "radiant" planet. This may be understood as having a high core temperature. Although controversial, there is also astrophysical opinion that a large body in elongated orbit is constantly tending toward circular orbit and this causes stresses in the body that could generate a good deal of heat. That their planet was gradually cooling may be indicated by Sitchin's interpretation of their colonizing Earth for the purpose of obtaining large quantities of gold for molecular seeding of their atmosphere with a reflective gold shield. Pertinent here is Harrington's confident statement to Sitchin that it is "a nice, good planet, could be surrounded by gases, probably has an atmosphere and could support life like ours". The sunlight level there might be quite different than on earth.

The Anunnaki were often depicted or sculpted with what seem to be gigantism. Is there any relationship between the Anunnaki and what we call the grays? The grays have large black eyes and they are sensitive to bright lights. The Anunnaki are depicted on Sumerian tablets and in Egypt hieroglyphics as human like and standing over seven feet tall. Either the grays are a different species from somewhere else, or they are androids for the Anunnaki. What we would call (AI) Artificial Intelligence made by a far superior race advanced thousands of years before man? If, however, the Anunnaki evolved on a radically different planet from earth under quite different conditions in which to adapt, why should they have turned out to be so similar to humans? Sitchin's answer is based on the coalitional event between the intruder planet Nibiru and the planet Tiamat, the residual part of which re-congealed into the Earth after being driven into the current earth orbit. That the two, or at least one, of the colliding planets was sufficiently developed to have evolved basic organic compounds, perhaps even basic life, the cross-seeding of everything from amino acids to more complicated organic compounds or even primitive organisms could account for the evolutionary similarity. The cross-seeding theory can account for the apparent relative ease with which the Anunnaki impinged their genes on the genes of Homo erectus.

The Anunnaki skill level 200,000 years ago is indicated by the recorded fact that in early trials they succeeded in crossing animal genes with Homo erectus genes they obtained living hybrids but never a satisfactory product which led them to modify Homo erectus genes with their advanced genes. We today have the technology to manipulate vegetable genes as well as animal genes to produce a hybrid stock. In fact, Monsanto has the corner on almost all hybrid vegetable seed and they sell it to the farmers for a fee. I am sure there was a lot of trial and error creating the perfect seed and the early man project as explained in the Sumerian text concerning the creation of man may have had the same problem with producing perfect man. The castaway may have been the early ape-man as a result of trial and error. It may also account for Greek and Egyptian mythology pictograms showing the mixture of Animals and early man. If our genome is estimated as 98% to 99% similar to the chimpanzee, how could there be a melding of the Homo erectus and Anunnaki genomes or impingement of the advanced code on the lesser advanced one detectable? I suggest that this is a complicated question probably answerable only by the geneticists open-minded enough to attack it. Advancements in this field are providing some spectacular results in many other fields of medical studies. They have confirmed certain genes that are not only odd, but should not even be in our DNA.

The Fox-P2 gene is a perfect example of this and ancestors of old tell us this was a gift from their gods. The resolution of that question should provide rich additional clues in itself and solid proof we are genetically different from prior species on earth when compared to ape-man. Recent scientific studies comparing Neanderthal to human and chimpanzee genomes showed that at multiple locations the Neanderthal DNA sequences matched chimpanzee DNA but not human.

CHAPTER 2

In the Beginning

According to a recent statement by the prominent Professor Steven Hawking[13], "God was not needed to create the Universe; the Big Bang was the result of the inevitable laws of physics and did not need God to spark the creation of the Universe, In fact, before the Big Bang there was nothing. No time or matter, therefore there was no God before the Big Bang".

That statement upset millions of religious believers around the world, contradicting the religious societies, as well as the Churches of many religions. But the real question is, "Is it true?" If there was nothing before the big bang, where and when did God come to be, did God come after the bang? Did he evolve over time to become the God we speak of within the religious communities, and if he did evolve, was it on some other planet which we humans call Heaven? After all, Heaven had to exist after the big bang? Perhaps Heaven was a planet and God came to be over time on that planet. I do not agree with Hawking's statement. As you keep reading, you will learn who God most likely is and how he is much more than we could possibly imagine. Yes, there is "ONE GOD" as you will learn in later chapters.

---

13   Stephen William Hawking, CH, CBE, FRS, FRSA English theoretical physicist, cosmologist

TIMING OF THE UNIVERSE

The earth is between 3 to 4 billion years old and our sun is about 4 .6 billion. Other suns in and out of our Milky Way are much older and planets circling around those suns are many billions of years older.

Quoting the book of Genesis: In the beginning God created the heavens and the earth. Now the earth was formless and empty, darkness was over the surface of the deep and the Spirit[14] of God was hovering over the waters. And God said, "Let there be light," and there was light. God saw that the light was good and he separated the light from the darkness. God called the light "day," and the darkness he called "night." And there was evening and there was morning—the first day. And God said, "Let there be a vault between the waters to separate water from water." ⁷ So God made the vault and separated the water under the vault from the water above it. And it was so. God called the vault "sky." And there was evening and there was morning, the second day. And God said, "Let the water under the sky be gathered to one place and let dry ground appear." And it was so. ¹⁰ God called the dry ground "land," and the gathered waters he called "seas." And God saw that it was good. Then God said, "Let the land produce vegetation: seed-bearing plants and trees on the land that bear fruit with seed in it, according to their various kinds." And it was so. The land produced vegetation: plants bearing seed according to their kinds and trees bearing fruit with seed in it according to their kinds. And God saw that it was good. And there was evening and there was morning—the third day.

And God said, "Let there be lights in the vault of the sky to separate the day from the night and let them serve as signs to mark sacred times and days and years, and let them be lights in the vault of the sky to give light on the earth." And it was so. God made two great lights the greater light to govern the day and the lesser light to govern

---

14   English word spirit (from Latin *spiritus* "breath")

the night. He also made the stars. God set them in the vault of the sky to give light on the earth, to govern the day and night and to separate light from the darkness. And God saw that it was good. And there was evening and there was morning the fourth day. And God said, "Let the water teem with living creatures and let birds fly above the earth across the vault of the sky." So God created the magnificent creatures of the sea and every living thing with which the water teems and that moves about in it, according to their kinds and every winged bird according to its kind. And God saw that it was good. God blessed them and said, "Be fruitful and increase in number and fill the water in the seas and let the birds increase on the earth. And there was evening and there was morning the fifth day. And God said, "Let the land produce living creatures according to their kinds: the livestock, the creatures that move along the ground and the wild animals, each according to its kind." And it was so. God made the wild animals according to their kinds, the livestock according to their kinds and all the creatures that move along the ground according to their kinds.

And God saw that it was good. Then God said, "Let us make mankind in our image, in our likeness, so that they may rule over the fish in the sea and the birds in the sky, over the livestock and all the wild animals and over all the creatures that move along the ground." So God created mankind in his own image, in the image of God he created them; male and female he created them. God blessed them and said to them, "Be fruitful and increase in number; fill the earth and subdue it. Rule over the fish in the sea and the birds in the sky and over every living creature that moves on the ground." Then God said, "I give you every seed-bearing plant on the face of the whole earth and every tree that has fruit with seed in it. They will be yours for food. And to all the beasts of the earth and all the birds in the sky and all the creatures that move along the ground everything that has the breath of life in it, I give every green plant for food", and it was so. God saw all that he had made and it was exceedingly good. And there was evening and there was morning the sixth day.

In the Jewish Torah, Lilith became Adam's first wife, who was created at the same time and from the same earth as Adam. This contrasts with Eve, who was created from one of Adam's ribs. The legend was significantly developed during the middle ages in the tradition of Aggadic Midrashim, the Zohar and Jewish mysticism. In the 13th Century writings of Rabbi Isaac ben Jacob ha-Cohen, for example, Lilith left Adam after she refused to become subservient to him and then would not return to the Garden of Eden after she mated with Archangel Samuel in the Book of Isaiah 34:13-15, "Her castles shall be overgrown with thorns, her fortresses with thistles and briers. She shall become an abode for jackals and a haunt for ostriches"

Nowhere does it say that God came to or ever stayed on earth. Yet we have written proof from the Sumerian text, the Egyptian text, the Mayan text, the Aztec text and India text that they lived with and co-existed with gods? There is no mention of gods in the Bible except one God who lived in heaven. I personally find that extremely odd that the Christian Bible would leave out all these gods that were a large part of history within many religions at the time.

Nowhere do the writings show comprehendible time as we know it today. In reality it is totally impossible for all this to have taken place in six earth days as stated in the Bible. As humans, we want to know answers that are fact and can be proven. It makes much more sense when you consider that it took time, a lot of time, for all this to happen. Especially when you consider that many parts of our universe are older than others and could not happen all at the same time like in Genesis. Remember, the sun was here before the earth, and the Milky Way was here long before our Sun in our solar system.

My position is that if the book of Genesis is true, then scientists are completely wrong, carbon dating is wrong, and everything in the universe is the same age, including Earth. If Genesis is wrong or was changed for some reason when written, then it makes more sense that we humans were a product of genetic manipulation by some superior entity known as God or gods of that time. Scientists around the world may be correct, or much more correct than the book of Genesis based on the DNA advancement projects. Perhaps the Genesis part of the Bible is fact when it says God created man. However it may have been the Sumerian gods. The Bible never tells us who God is, just that he is God. The Bible, as any book, must have a beginning and religion must have a structure and belief system to exist. Being a realist and human, both theories cannot be correct.

The Sumerian civilization is older than the Bible and much more likely to be correct in the fact that the Elohim (those who came from above) seeded earth, as stated in their written text on clay tablets 2000 years before anyone ever wrote the Old Testament. The Torah was written in 600 BCE by Jews leaving the same reign as the Sumerians and they surely heard and read the stories of the area and carried the information with them and recorded it in what we know as the Torah which preceded the Catholic Bible by some 650 years.

The Babylonian, Sumerian, Assyrians, god finished his work within the span of six clay tablets. The last and seventh tablet exalted the handiwork and greatness of the deity's work.

Thus, the comparison must be made that the seven days of creation found in the Bible, borrowed its theme from the Jewish Torah; and the Torah got it from the Babylonians and them from the Sumerians. The sixth clay tablet tells how they made man. The seventh clay tablet tells how the Anunnaki gave praise to the creator of everything on earth, including man. The seventh day is the day they rested. Also, the seventh day is Saturday. Sunday (beginning of the week) was the day of worship in Rome to the mystical god Mithras[15] who was a Persian god.

Now knowing that there were two stories concerning the creation concept. The Sumerian concept and Genesis and knowing the Bible was written some 2000 years after the Sumerian tablets, which were the basis for the original story, written slightly differently, it becomes perplexing to distinguish which is more true, like the orange turning into an apple after being told from one person to another over time.

The earth took thousands of years just to chill down enough for basic life to grow and evaluation of microscopic life form to mutate into both land and sea animals. When comparing the age of earth at 3 to 4 billion years old and the formation of man according to the Anunnaki, there is a massive amount of time that passed in order for everything other than man to evolve and adapt to earth's environments.

The Sumerians did not write about the beginning of time because it was already there, but they did write about how we humans were formed and how the trees and fruit bearing trees were planted by the Anunnaki, as well as the seeds of earth.

This would also include primates which were here before man and were engineered by the Anunnaki using both primate genes and Anunnaki genes. What we humans call genetic engineering. This would answer perfectly the part in the Bible where God said "let us make man in our image" The use of us is plural, which would suggest that God was speaking to others and not by himself. Primates did not look like Anunnaki, but they were close genetically to be able

---

15   Mithras is an Old Persian god worshiped by the Romans BC. (aka) the bull slayer.

to manipulate their DNA to be more like Homo sapiens (modern man).

The question I have is: Who are and how did the Anunnaki come to be, and how old is their civilization compared to ours?

RELIGIONS OF THE WORLD

With over 40 religious groups in the world today, they provide hope and something to believe in. Either it is their god or themselves.

Listed are but a few of the major religions throughout the world today.

• **Catholic religion:** *2.6 Billion Followers*

God the father, Jesus Christ the son and the Holy Spirit, or ghost. These three deities together form the Christian Trinity.

• **Hindu religion**: *900 Million Followers*

Lord Brahma brings forth the creation and represents the creative principle of the Supreme Being. Lord Vishnu maintains the universe and represents the eternal principle of preservation. Lord Shiva represents the principle of dissolution and recreation. These three deities together form the Hindu Trinity.

• **Buddhism religion:** *360 Million Followers*

Buddhism does not believe in the existence of a God who created the universe. As per Lord Buddha, one should emphasize on the practical ways of life, which will help a person in attaining enlightenment. However, at the same time, Buddha did not rule out the existence of a God or Gods altogether. With the growth and spread of Buddhism, local deities and religious practices were included in it. Today, Tibetan Buddhist cosmology talks about a large number of 'Divine Beings' believed to be representative of the psychic life. One of the six realms of the Tibetan cosmology is the realm of gods who must take birth on earth as humans to attain enlightenment.

• **Islam religion:** *1.3 Billion Followers*

The single most influential belief in Islam and arguably the central theme of Islam, is that there is only one God. The name of God is *Allah*, which is simply Arabic for "the (*al*) God (*Ilah*)." The term is related to *Elohim*, the Hebrew word for God. According to the Qur'an, Allah "created man from a clot of blood" at the same time he created the *jinn* from fire. Humans are the greatest of all creatures, created with free will for the purpose of obeying and serving God.

• **Christian Science religion:** *400 Thousand Followers*

Heaven is "not a locality, but a divine state of mind in which all the manifestations of mind are harmonious and immortal."

• **Judaism religion:** *14 Million Followers*

One God, Yahweh (YHVH). In days of old this God had many names including Elohim. Remember, Elohim was used and written by the Assyrians to convey the Gods they were connected to, those that came from above (Elohim).

• **Mormon religion:** *12.2 Million Followers*

God the Father, the Son Jesus Christ and the Holy Ghost are three separate individual beings.

• **Taoism religion:** *394 Million Followers*

No supreme being, no God. Pantheism - the Tao pervades all. Yin-yang - opposites make up a unity. Purpose is inner harmony, peace and longevity. Achieved by living in accordance with the Tao.

Out of all the religions, the Christian religion is the largest with 2.6 Billion followers and growing every day around the world. The Catholic Church is said to be the richest entity on earth. They along with Constantine[16] decided what books would make up the entire Catholic Bible. Leaving out dozens of books written about God and Jesus. I find it ironic that this religion came about during the rule of Emperor Gaius Julius Caesar Augustus who ruled alone from 306-337AD The Christians were persecuted for centuries until Emperor Flavius Valerius Aurelius Constantinus Augustus also known as Constantine I or Saint Constantine, was Roman Emperor converted to Christianity. He was well known for being the first Roman emperor to convert to Christianity because he saw a cross in the sky before a battle, of which he won. He attributed the win to the Christian God and not only converted, but created the counsel of the new church and gave them full control. In effect, he created the new Rome with the Catholic Church at its center. Legend has it that after converting, God, or his angels gave Constantine a secret weapon or plans to make such. It was called Greek Fire,[17] and it was devastating during its use. In fact, it could not be duplicated even with today's technology, as we have no plans from which to work.

If you are familiar with the Catholic Church, then you should be aware they were and may still be, the most powerful in the world. A chronicled example of their power included, but not limited to:

- The Spanish inquisition, where thousands were killed for being non-believers.

- The Templars crusade to rule over Israel and wipe out the Muslim religion.

---

16   Roman Emperor Constantine the Great (reigned 306–337), Christianity became a dominant religion of the Roman Empire.

17   Greek fire was an incendiary weapon used by the Byzantine Empire

- The entire middle ages where the church tortured and killed thousands of non-believers, or anyone who challenged the Church.

- The burning of witches and warlocks in Salem, USA (Protestant Catholic).

The fact is, the Catholic Church was an extension of the Roman control disguised under Christian Religion. This is completely the opposite of what Jesus Christ taught while he was alive and speaking of his belief in God and Heaven. I am not against the Catholic Church, and everyone makes mistakes, even them. For me, I have a difference of opinion based on the foundation, control and wealth of the Catholic Church. I tend to respect more Mother Theresa, a woman of God, who possessed nothing but her Bible and some other books which she prized and helped thousands of the poor and sick throughout her entire life and asking for nothing in return. That is what I call unselfish true love, being one with the soul, spirit, of her God. She was the female figure of Jesus Christ in modern times.

CHAPTER 3

The Gods of Old

Of the 40 religions, today, 94% have a God. Although the names are different for some, the belief in a supreme being is always prevalent. Below is a small list of but a few gods and their names throughout history. Starting with the ones that are perhaps the most beneficial, as it establishes the belief in gods from the first written records by the Assyrians and preserved today.

1. <u>The Anunnaki (Elohim) those that came from above</u>

From the beginning of time, there were gods. The Assyrians spoke of gods in the tablets of books and the legend of Gilgamesh.[18] This is also known as the oldest poem, or story written in history and is preserved on 12 clay tablets today. The story revolves around a relationship between Gilgamesh and his close male companion, Enkidu. Enkidu is a wild man created by the gods as Gilgamesh's equal to distract him from oppressing the citizens of Uruk. Together they undertake dangerous quests that incur the displeasure of the gods. Firstly, they journey to the Cedar Mountain of Lebanon to defeat Humbaba, its monstrous guardian. Later they kill the bull of

---

18   Gilgamesh is a demigod of superhuman strength who built the city walls of Uruk to defend his people from external threats, and travelled to meet the sage Utnapishtim, who had survived the Great Deluge.

Heaven that the Goddess Ishtar had sent to punish Gilgamesh for spurning her advances.

It should also be noted that the great flood of Noah and the flood of Gilgamesh are remarkably similar in tale. However, the Gilgamesh story predates the Bible account by some 2000 years.

2. <u>The Gods of India</u>

To name a few: Brahma - Deva • Vishnu • Shiva • Rama • Krishna • Ganesha • Murugan • Hanuman • Indra • Surya Brahma is the Hindu God (deva) of creation and one of the Trimurti, the others being Vishnu and Shiva. According to the Brahma Purana, he is the father of Mānuand from Mānu all human beings are descended. The most famous of the divine incarnation is Rama, whose life is depicted in the Ramayana and Krishna, whose life is depicted in the Mahābhārata and the Bhagavata Purana. The Bhagavad Gita, which contains the spiritual teachings of Krishna, is one of the most widely read scriptures in Hinduism.

One story is in the Mahābhārata tells of a great battle, The Great War or epic begins with the established need for sacrifice in order that true prosperity (Sri) might be restored here on Earth. The Goddess Earth is oppressed by demons and evil. Visnu and several other gods descend from above to assist the Goddess Visnu. Krsna, friend and cousin to the Pandava brothers, who are fathered by gods for whom they become earthly assistants.

The weapons that are mentioned in this battle are extremely futuristic. Flying craft, lasers, sleep gas, arrows that are heat seeking to the target and hand held bombs. How is it possible that warfare weapons used today may have been used thousands of years ago? The only logical answer has to be from a civilization far more advanced than humans at the time of this war. Could this be proof of the Anunnaki

(Elohim) that came to earth from above battling others which may have been alien invaders from somewhere else in the universe or their own kind who opposed them? Keep in mind this battle happened thousands of years ago.

3. The Greek Gods

<u>Aphrodite</u>: Goddess of love and beauty.

<u>Apollo</u>: God of music, healing, plague prophecies, poetry and archery; associated with light, truth and the sun

<u>Ares</u>: God of war, bloodlust, violence, manly courage and civil order. The son of Zeus and Hera,

<u>Artemis</u>: Virgin Goddess of the hunt, wilderness, wild animals, childbirth and plague. In later times, she became associated with the moon

<u>Athena</u>: Goddess of wisdom, warfare, battle strategy, heroic endeavor, handicrafts and reason

<u>Demeter</u>: Goddess of agriculture, horticulture, grain and harvest. Demeter is a daughter of Cronus and Rhea and sister of Zeus

<u>Dionysus</u>: God of wine, parties and festivals, madness, drunkenness and pleasure at forever young.

<u>Hades </u>or <u>Pluto</u>: King of the Underworld and God of the dead and the hidden wealth of the Earth.

<u>Hephaestus</u>: Crippled God of fire, metalworking, stonemasonry, sculpture and volcanism.

<u>Hera</u>: Queen of marriage, women, childbirth, heirs, kings and empires. She is the wife of Zeus and daughter of Cronus

<u>Hermes</u>: God of travel, messengers, trade, thievery, cunning wiles, language, writing, diplomacy, athletics and animal husbandry. He is the messenger of the Gods,

<u>Hestia</u>: Virgin Goddess of the hearth, home and cooking. She is a daughter of Rhea and Cronus and sister of Zeus

<u>Poseidon</u>: God of the sea, rivers, floods, droughts, earthquakes and the creator of horses; known as the "Earth Shaker".

<u>Zeus</u>: The king of the Gods, the ruler of Mount Olympus and the God of the sky, weather, thunder, law, order and fate. He is the youngest son of Cronus and Rhea

These are just the main Gods for the Greek and Romans. The numbers of demigods in addition to the Gods of the Greek Titians included:

4. **Roman Gods**

Apollo	Greek (Apollo)
Ceres	Greek (Demeter)
Diana	Greek (Artemis)
Juno	Greek (Hera)
Jupiter	Greek (Zeus)
Mars	Greek (Ares)
Mercury	Greek (Hermes)
Minerva	Greek (Athena)
Neptune	Greek (Poseidon)
Venus	Greek (Aphrodite)
Vesta	Greek (Hestia)
Vulcan	Greek (Hephaestus)

An interesting fact is that the Romans adopted these gods as their own in an effort to please all the gods. In fact, all the lands they conquered, they adopted the gods of their captors. They changed some of the names to suit their needs and to please the gods they had already paid homage to prior to adding new gods to their list. Their perception was, the more gods on their side, the more likely their success both in battle and in Rome itself. In fact, Mithras, (minor god) in the Roman Empire was worshipped and popular with soldiers. His birthday was December 25th. When the Catholic Church was trying to figure out the birth of Jesus Christ, the Church chose the same day as Mithras? This was done to make both the Christians and the multi God believer's happy. In fact, many prior gods and demigods claim the same birthday of December 25th.

Here is a list of some and there are even more not included in this list:

- Horus (c. 3000 BCE) Born of Virgin

- Osiris (c. 3000 BCE)

- Attis of Phrygia (c.1400 BCE)

- Krishna (c. 1400 BCE)

- Zoroaster/Zarathustra (c. 1000 BCE)

- Mithras of Persia (c. 600 BCE) Born of virgin

- Heracles (c. 800 BCE)

- Dionysus (c. 186 BCE)

- Tammuz (c. 400 BCE)

- Adonis (c. 200 BCE)

- Hermes

- Bacchus

- Prometheus

Something to take note of: the birth of Mithras is within the same timing of the creation of the Jewish Torah. It should also be noted that the Jews leaving Egypt casted a gold bull for worship on their exodus. Mithras may relate to the story of Gilgamesh, who killed the bull of heaven. In later stories, Mithras is known as the bull slayer and the Jews sacrificed a pure red heifer to God, up until a few hundred years ago.

According to today's astrologers and astrophysicists, the sighting of the star of Bethlehem was in early September and not December. Perhaps that is why I have always said to my children and grandchildren, "Every day is Christmas, and you do not need a specific day to give someone a gift". Maybe by reading this book, they will understand my statement?

5. <u>Mayan Gods:</u>

The ancient Mayan lived in the sub-tropical area of Mesoamerica that is now Guatemala, the Yucatan peninsula of Mexico, western Honduras, Belize and El Salvador. They flourished in the classic period of Mesoamerican history when they were living in city-states characterized by strong kings, mightily impressive astronomical and mathematical calculations, including an accurate calendar with a concept of zero.

Ah Puch The God of death

Chac Benevolent fertility God

Kinich Ahau Maya sun God.

Kukulcan The feathered snake, civilization and rain

Ix Chel Rainbow, earth and moon Goddess

Ixtab Goddess of the hanged and suicide.

I have listed different religious groups who had many gods. Of course, there are many more Gods throughout history. My intent was and is, to show how in the days of old, people of earlier times worshiped many diverse gods. They made offerings to all of them, be it blood sacrifice or food or metals, in an attempt to please the gods of their time and gain favor.

Of all the gods of time, the one that stands out is the God of Abraham. The Catholics, Jews, Muslims, Mormons and many of the 40 plus religions in existence today believe in this one God. If you crunch the numbers, that means approximately 4.2 billion people of the 6 billion plus humans on earth believe there is one almighty God. All the others gods have disappeared through time with the exception of a few.

The Jews believed in one God the longest, going back to Abraham. It was not until Jesus Christ[19] came to be that the belief in one God came into existence for Christians.

According to the Bible, which is complicated to understand in the first place, Jesus was born of a virgin (Mary)and the wise men (Magi), were a group of distinguished foreigners who were said to have visited Jesus after his birth, led by a sign from the heavens, the star of Bethlehem.

---

19   Jesus Christ 7–2 BC/BCE to 30–36 AD/CE), also referred to as Jesus of Nazareth, is the central figure of Christianity, whom the teachings of most Christian denominations hold to be the Son of God,

The miracles of Jesus started when he was a child and continued until the day he was crucified on the cross. In this period of Roman rule, the death of people on the cross was common, easy, very effective and literally thousands were killed the same way. To them Christ was just another person who would die the same way as the others before him. Jesus was perhaps the only human person on earth that was most visible to thousands of people at the time. His teachings were specific to his God and heaven among many other teachings and speeches he made during his short life span. At the time he was born, it was Rome's golden age and they worshiped many gods. The Jews worshiped (Elohim)[20] God; The Muslims worshiped the same God under a different name (Allah). Seeing the suffering and persecution during his younger years, he too was looking for something to believe in that could unite all people. Imagine if you were living in this time period where Romans controlled everything. Their gods were many and more powerful than just one God.

Jesus' teachings were a glimmer of hope and salvation to many who followed him. Even today we see thousands looking for reason and hope. We all believe that there is and must be a superior being somewhere out there, who will save us in the end. It was no different in the times of Jesus.

There are hundreds of books and papers that talk about Jesus Christ being the son of God, but the real question is why he was more influential than the others like Buddha, Muhammad, Krishna and more The Muslim's speak of Jesus as a prophet like Muhammad and others of their religion. However, Jesus Christ was the only one who performed miracles that defied understanding today. This may be the single reason why he is revered as a reincarnation or equal to God, especially within Catholic and Christian religions with some 2.6 billion followers today.

---

20 Elohim was a Jewish name for God; the same name used in the Sumerian tablets, "Those who came from above".

CHAPTER 4

Where is Heaven

We do not know where heaven is, or do we? I always found it fascinating that some scholars say there are more stars in the universe than there are grains of sand in all the world beaches. Now everyone has heard that there are trillions of stars in the universe and billions in the Milky Way alone. Mind you, we are talking about stars and not planets within a star system. In our own star system, we have eight planets not counting Pluto. Just one is the salvation for mankind, Earth. Some say Earth is somewhere between 3 to 4.6 billion years old and they are not really sure about that. So how old are the other planets that circle their star?

A star is a sun and not a planet. Our sun is a star, one of a billion, if not, trillions in the universe. Looking up into a clear night, with no lights around for miles and one will be amazed at what can be seen. I remember one night sitting on a hill in the middle of an open dark field and being shocked for the first time in my life. Being a city boy, I never genuinely saw the sky in total darkness. I never knew there were so many stars in the universe. They were always there, but I could not see all of them under the city lights. It was like someone poured a fifty pound bag of salt in the sky above me. I say this because sometimes in life we cannot see the whole picture due to our surroundings. Like the wind, you know it's there, but you cannot see it. You see the trees move due to wind, but you cannot see wind even though you know it is there. For me, the memory of all those stars that night has stayed in my brain forever. Looking up at the stars on a clear dark night, one has to wonder what is out there and are we really alone?

Where is heaven in this massive cluster of stars and galaxies? This is only what our eyes can see. Remember, for every star you see, there are nine more you cannot see with the naked eye. Try it sometime. Go away from all lighting in the middle of a field and just look up. You too will be amazed at the universe around you. While you are looking up at billions of suns, try to locate Heaven. It is virtually impossible for many reasons. One reason is, we do not know if heaven is even in our universe. Science propounds the fact that there may be more than one Universe as described in string theory[21], multidimensional Universes existing in a different dimension based on the possibility there may be as many as 11 dimensions. We humans only see two dimensions and our brain reconstructs it to three dimensions. The other dimensions are as of yet unknown. Heaven is a common religious, cosmological, mythological, or metaphysical term for the physical or transcendent place from which heavenly beings (such as a God, angels, the jinn and sky deities or venerated ancestors) originate, are enthroned or inhabit. It is commonly believed that heavenly beings can descend to earth or incarnate, and that earthly beings can ascend to Heaven in the afterlife or in exceptional cases, enter Heaven alive.

Is heaven a one star system? Is it a planet which we cannot see with the naked eye? Is it in the Milky Way galaxy? Maybe it is in another galaxy, a tiny little dot in the sky. I mentioned that you cannot see planets that circle around those stars that you see in the night

---

21 String theory is an active research framework in particle physics that attempts to reconcile quantum mechanics and general relativity. It is a contender for a theory of everything.

sky. N.A.S.A. cannot see them either, but we know they are out there. Kind of like the wind I mentioned above. As recently as 2011, scientists have found planets and predict there may be billions more. Some are earth-like, but most not. They call it the goldilocks zone. So far, they are light years away from us.

If there is a God, where is his home out in the vast universe? How does he travel? We may never know, but there are some clues that were left here on earth. Chapter one spoke of the Anunnaki (Elohim) coming from the sky. The evidence is on hundreds of clay tablets that are the oldest writings known to man. The Mayans and the Incas had vast knowledge of the stars and even created a calendar that is more correct than our best clocks today. They foretold of future events and movements of the universe without any modern instruments or telescopes. Even today scientists are baffled by how they were able to do this with the little they had. Someone had to teach them. Someone had to teach the pyramid builders how to use mathematics to build the massive structures they made that still stand over three thousand years later.

The Greeks also built massive complex buildings both to their gods and houses of worship. But let's for a brief moment let's focus on just three civilizations that stand out the most. The Egyptians, Mayan and Aztecs. Although they were not neighbors, they shared knowledge of the stars and the universe around them. Why? What was the reason for learning the distant stars and what did it help them achieve? Someone or something taught them this information. Think about it. How do humans learn things they cannot comprehend? How did they know what they were looking at other than a million small pricks of light in the night sky? What did it mean?

Some of the information may have been passed down from generation to generation and some may have been lost in time. I can say with absolute certainty, we do not possess the knowledge that was known thousands of years ago. They knew where Orion's Belt was and built their temples to mimic the same pattern in the sky during their time. Why Orion's Belt? Why not some other star systems like the North Star or visible planets within our close solar system like Mars, Mercury, Venus, and Uranus? Why a group of stars way out in space?

It is my belief and the accepted belief of ancient alien astronaut theorist that if you are going to interpret the information at hand, you have to ask the straightforward questions first. Why did the builders of old design all their massive structures relating to Orion's Belt? The answer has to be, or at least to me Orion's Belt solar system has a definite connection with the Elohim or those that came from above, or it is heaven itself.

The Assyrians spoke of it in their writings. The Egyptians designed their pyramids in line with it. The Aztecs and Mayans built their pyramids exactly like those pyramids; only the base and design were slightly different. They all reference this single group of stars out of billions in the sky. Why is this area of the stars so influential? Is it possible that this may be heaven as described in the Bible? Scientists claim that there are billions of stars in the Milky Way galaxy and billions of galaxies in the universe and perhaps, even more we do not see.

Just to clarify, a star is a Sun and it is possible that around every sun there may be planets like ours. In 1961, Frank Drake wrote down an equation for the chance of a contactable alien civilization from another planet in the Milky Way Galaxy. This is known as the Drake Equation[22]. If using the Drake equation and the least number being one, the possibility of life on other planets in the universe even at 1% would still be millions of earth like planets that may have intelligent life.

---

22   The Drake equation: $N = R^* \cdot f_p \cdot n_e \cdot f_l \cdot f_i \cdot f_c \cdot L$

In the Bible it states that Enoch[23] was taken to heaven and instructed by God to learn from his Angels. And after many years, Enoch was returned to Earth with knowledge far beyond any human. In the Koran, Mohammed was said to do the same. Both of these humans came back to earth with vastly more knowledge than any man on earth.

One must question how it is possible that Enoch and Mohammed could possibly leave earth's atmosphere if they were not protected by something and how they got there in the first place. Enoch "walked with God: and he was not; for God took him", (Genesis 5:22-29) suggesting he did not experience the mortal death ascribed to Adam's other descendants. Enoch lived 365 years which is extremely short in the context of his peers. The Bible does not say that Enoch died, only that he was taken by God.

If the Bible is the word of God, then one must accept that Enoch was taken off the earth somehow, went somewhere and returned to earth many years later. In those days, humans lived for hundreds of years and today no one is older than 120 years old. Some literary critics explain these extreme ages as ancient mistranslations that converted the word "month" to "year" mistaking lunar cycles for solar ones. This would turn an age of 969 "years" into a more reasonable 969 lunar months, or 78½ years of the Metonic cycle. However, the text says that Arpachshad (son of Shem) **Note:** (Shem is mentioned in Sumerian tablets) fathered Shelah at 35 years of age. If that is taken to mean 35 months, then Arpachshad was a father before turning three years of age. In addition, the first chapters of Genesis distinguish solar cycles of years from lunar cycles of months. (Genesis 1:14–16; 7:11. If evolution allowed humans to live hundreds of years of age back then, what changed in our DNA to cause it to stop? God said no man shall live past 120 years of age. God had to do something to

---

23   Enoch is described as the great[x4] grandson of Adam (through Seth) Note: Seth is mentioned in the Sumerian Clay Tablets.

our genetic makeup to cause this change to happen and that would be incorporated in our DNA.

No scientists alive today can explain how it is possible to live for as long as our elders did, nor can they locate the gene responsible for turning on or off age within humans. Only recently have scientists found six genes that they think are connected to age and are trying to figure out how they turn on or off. Some day they may be able to, but for now they just do not know.

THE GREAT FLOOD

According to the Bible, God told Noah to collect two of every animal on earth. If you think about this, it would be virtually impossible, as he would have had to travel the world to collect every species on earth. In 1996 on the Arctic island of Spaldart, scientists have collected thousands of the DNA samples from animals and man. They have also collected seed from every plant and tree on earth in an effort to preserve them in the event of a catastrophic disaster. The project is called frozen Ark project. If technology allows us to do this today, is it possible that a race of higher beings far more advanced than us would have been able to do the same thousands of years ago.

This could answer the question as to how Noah was able to collect two of every animal on earth. This also brings up the question as to how they were stored for 40 days. Remember that Noah was from the Middle East, and many animals although found in Africa would not account for the hundreds that were found in other parts of the world. Somehow, he was to collect two of every animal on earth and transport them to the Ark. If one is to consider this, he had to have help from more than just a few people. Far more noteworthy is: various types of animals were all over the globe and not found in the Middle East, yet Noah was to collect two of every creature on earth. Did he collect insects too?

The Bible is a record of time and what happened within that time and what will happen in the future. Yes, it is complicated to understand and still being discussed by many scholars throughout the world today. No one knows what the span of time is between chapters of the Bible as explained in previous chapters. God made everything in six days and rested on the seventh. The question is, did time exist back then as we see it today? Our concept of time is new, and was not a part of the past. It is man created. My position on this chapter of a stairway to heaven is the fact that what a person does in his human life here on earth, such as helping others and unselfish love for mankind, will allow him or her to be judged in favor of deserving a higher level of grace from the Universal God. Greed and selfishness will lower his or her chances of reaching heaven as we know it. This is the bases of all religions.

The Catholic Church calls this limbo or purgatory, which may or may not exist. Many religions are constructed to create fear to control mankind for the purpose of keeping humans in check and restricting free thought and free will through persecution. Examples are do good and go to heaven, be bad and go to hell. Donate money to your church and help it grow. Note The Catholic Church is the richest private entity in the world today. It has land, money, power, influence, its own banking system and in Rome it is its own Government within Italy. It owns massive collections of priceless art, gold and documents dating back thousands of years, all of which is off limits to the public as well as church members.

CHAPTER 5

Science Challenges The Bible

DEBATED FOR HUNDREDS OF YEARS, WHAT ARE THE FACTS?

The prior chapters gave some idea of my questions and some facts based on written tablets over 6000 years old. Keep in mind the clay tablets are older than the Pyramids. As you have learned, the Sumerians who lived in Mesopotamia which was later changed to Sumer and Persia is now known as Iraq. They were the first humans to document a variety of laws, government, military and everyday involvement with what they called their gods, which were known as the Anunnaki. You read in prior chapters that according to the Sumerians tablet the Anunnaki created man and women, and the Bible claims God made Adam then Eve.

The Bible, the Jewish Torah and the Dead Sea Scrolls introduce a woman who was made before Eve and her name was Lilith.[24] Although the Christian Bible says extremely little about Lilith, some of the other scripts claim the following story:

- God created Lilith and Adam both at the same time. Adam felt he was superior to Lilith, and because of this,

---

24   The Sumerian she-demons *lili*

he insisted on always taking the top position during sexual intercourse. However, Lilith refused to consider herself anything besides equal to Adam. They were, after all, created as equals and Lilith believed she should take the top position, too. Adam refused and told Lilith, "You are fit only to be in the bottom position." Lilith, realizing neither she nor Adam would willingly change their mind, spoke the secret name of YHWH. Transformed into a demon, Lilith flew away from the garden, leaving Adam behind. And since she had gone without eating from the Tree of the Knowledge of Good and Evil, Lilith would remain immortal.

- God watched Adam in the garden and said, "It is not good for the man to be alone. I will make a helper suitable for him." To avoid a repeat of the Lilith debacle, God decided this time to create a mate who was submissive. So God put Adam to sleep and removed one of his ribs, using it to create Eve. Upon meeting Eve, Adam said, "This is now bone of my bones and flesh of my flesh; she shall be called 'woman,' for she was taken out of man."

In some accounts, Lilith mates with the archangel Samuel, further transforming her into a succubus[25]. In others, Lilith is the evil serpent in the garden who tempts Eve into eating from The Tree of the Knowledge of Good and Evil, so (unlike the immortal Lilith) Adam, Eve and their offspring could die. And there lies a problem with the Bible version concerning the creation of Man and Woman.

As stated in Genesis 1:27; "God created man in his own image, in the image of God created he him; male and female created he them." In

---

25   Succubus may take a form of a beautiful young girl, but closer inspection may reveal deformities such as, having bird-like claws or serpentine tails It is said that the act of sexually penetrating a succubus is akin to entering a cavern of ice.

this verse, God creates man and woman at the same time. However, in Genesis 2, we read that Adam is alone.

Genesis 2:18; The Lord God said, "It is not good for the man to be alone. I will make a helper suitable for him." So, after already having a mate created at the same time that he was, Adam is alone in Genesis 2. Then the Bible tells us that God made Adam's wife from his rib.

Lilith was banished forever from the garden by God, and mentioned once more in the Bible.

Something else to question is the children of Eve. Eve had two sons, Cain and Abel. Cain killed his brother Abel and wandered in the desert. Eve had a total of nine children. So how is it possible that Cain should come across a woman from another village that he married and bore children? The Bible says Cain married his sister whom he did not know in later years. The problem is, there were only Eve's children on earth according to the Bible account. Is it possible, there were other humans living at the same time who were not offspring of Eve? The Bible does not clarify this dilemma. So was it incest, within the nine children or offspring of Lilith that these other from another village were from? It only mentions her by name and village. Their son was Enoch. This can be found in Genesis 4:16, Cain settled down and married his sister *Awan*, who bore his first son, the first *Enoch*, approximately 196 years after the creation of Adam. Cain then establishes the first city, naming it after his son, builds a house, and lives there until it collapses on him, killing him in the same year that Adam dies.

Back in a previous chapter, The Roman Emperor Constantine the Great also known as Saint Constantine created a council of Christian rulers and titled them as such in an effort to create order and control? The emperor had a direct hand in choosing what went in and what went out when putting the Bible together. Constantine and co-Emperor Licinius issued the Edict of Milan in 313, which proclaimed tolerance of all religions throughout the empire. Of course, we all know that Christianity was the dominant religion and the council (Catholic Church) made sure it held the power and control of Christians around the world. Ever ask yourself why the Vatican State is in Rome? Even today, it answers to no one as an independently governed country within a country.

To this very day, women are considered inferior to man. Yes, woman's liberation helped make them more equal in the 20th century, but are they as equal in other parts of the world? I think not. They are still stoned and killed every day in the Middle East and most cultures still regard them less than man.

In my opinion, the Sumerian tablet scripts may have gotten it right when they say the Anunnaki (gods) created man and woman by virtue of manipulating and mixing their genetic DNA with what we call early man (Homo erectus).

Here is why I say this:

Neanderthal Genome sequencing yields surprising results and opens a new door to future studies

The veil of mystery surrounding our extinct hominid cousins the Neanderthals, has been at least partially lifted to reveal surprising results. Scientists with the U.S. Department of Energy's Lawrence Berkeley National Laboratory (Berkeley Lab) and the Joint Genome Institute (JGI) have sequenced genomic DNA from fossilized Neanderthal bones. Their results show that the genomes of modern humans and Neanderthals are at least 99.5-percent identical, but despite this genetic similarity, and despite the two species having cohabitated in the same geographic region for thousands of years, there is no evidence of any significant crossbreeding between the two. Based on these early results, Homo sapiens and Homo Neanderthals last shared a common ancestor approximately 700,000 years ago.

This is the most fascinating part: comparing Neanderthal to human and chimpanzee genomes showed that at multiple locations the Neanderthal DNA sequences matched chimpanzee DNA, but not human. If Homo sapiens or Neanderthal were genetically infused with DNA from a race of people not from earth such as the Anunnaki then neither would be a perfect match. Our blood has what is known as an RH factor. It is either negative or positive. It is also called the monkey gene.

Explanation:

- The **Rh (Rhesus) blood group system,** (including the **Rh factor**) is one of thirty current human blood group systems. Clinically, it is the most significant blood group system after A.B.O. An individual either has or does not have the *"Rhesus factor"* on the surface of their red blood cells.

- This term strictly refers only to the most immunogenic D antigen of the Rh blood group system, or the Rh- blood group system. The status is usually indicated by Rh positive (Rh+ does have the D antigen) or Rh negative.

Here is information you may not have known:

- The RH negative blood factor, also known as Blue Blood is in only 15 % of humans, and several presidents, including Barak Obama are RH negative. Odd, right? Rh negative people are also usually red-haired, sensitive to light, have higher IQ, lower body temperature and have blue, hazel or green eyes. They also may be immune to the AIDS virus as well as a host of other diseases. Could this be the cause as stated in the Bible Genesis: 6; where the sons (angels) of God mated with the daughters of man and inadvertently infused the offspring with Anunnaki genes or blood?

- RH negative blood has no connection to the Rhesus's monkey gene. Even scientists and Doctors are puzzled as to why some people have the plus and negative RH factor, and they do not know where the different blood types came from.

So in conclusion, if the God of the Bible made man and woman, their blood would be exactly the same in all factors. If someone such as the Anunnaki infused their DNA in early man, be it Homo sapiens or Neanderthal, which were blood related to monkey, or whatever you wish to call apes, or early-man back then, why do we have so many different types of blood factors A-B-O, plus the RH factor either positive or negative? The Bible claims one man and one woman were made in his image, or at least man was.

So do you see where I am going with this? We have to give credence to the obscure possibility that someone did something to human DNA and blood to cause the differences in all of us, pertaining to blood types and DNA mismatches with any monkey on earth. I believe we are not direct descendants of monkeys, and Darwin's theory of man was never specifically stated in his book directly.

Ask yourself this one question "Why didn't monkeys develop a smart brain like humans?"

Or to put it another way "Why is man the smartest thing on earth?" The answer is straightforward, something or someone jumpstarted humans to develop faster than evolution would allow. Monkeys are still stupid compared to man, are they not? Also monkeys were here first. Man came much later in the timeline.

We humans have 252 genes[26] of 35,000 plus that scientists say are entirely unknown and foreign, as well as the fact that they do not know what they are for or do within our DNA. Science goes on to say that 97% of our DNA is considered junk DNA with no known use or purpose. Only 3% of the known DNA has a known purpose which turns on or off different functions during and after human development. These 252 genes are not shared with any other life form on earth. It will take our scientists another 30 years to complete 50% of the genome strand project.

Here is another fact to ponder, it is said what we use only 10% of our brain. No one knows what the other 90% is for or what it does. Ever wonder why?

I do not dispute the existence of GOD. In fact, the Bible is correct about God and the creation of the Universe. But in my opinion, our understanding of God is entirely wrong based on what we were taught through most religions. In fact, God is more than anyone came ever imagine. To know the true God, we must first look at the past. Science only recently discovered in the last century correlation's between the Bible and archeology findings. Many of the stories are being confirmed using modern science. Some of the problems scientists' encounters are difficult to fathom or comprehend based on our understanding of how things are supposed to work.

Everything they know is what was taught and learned through modern knowledge and technology. With all our knowledge and understanding, we are not sure how the Pyramids were built, the Mayan temples, Inca temples, Stone Henge, or even how the famous Crystal Skull was made. And those are but a few of the many structures and artifacts found around the world. How were stone blocks weighing more than 50 or 100 tons moved by primitive man with homemade tools? How were chambers in the temple of the

---

26   US Genome project

pyramids aligned with celestial stars? In fact, almost every structure created and built by our ancestor's point to a group of stars we call Pleiades or Orion's belt, which are both in the same constellation. Why? What did they know that we or not aware of today? Orion's Belt was named after a Greek demigod in eight BC. Orion was the mighty hunter with super human strength, who garnished a brass club. His father was Poseidon. Sirius, (the brightest star in the night sky) and Orion represent Isis and Osiris in Egypt mythology.

Why is NASA looking for life on other planets in our tiny solar system? Why do they leave plagues on the moon and mars, are they expecting someone other than humans to retrieve them? What do they know? Would they even tell us if they did, or hide it like all the UFO sightings and abduction claims throughout the world?

According to an Asian intelligence agency, reports that a combined fleet operation between the US and China has been going on, a full combat operation against what are said to be a "highly unfriendly extra-terrestrial threat."

The verifications of the fleet operations have been many however; there have been no confirmations from the US side, though the ships have been seen by commercial vessels offshore. The true nature of both the threat and the extent of the multinational military force used are beyond any known classification level.

UNCONFIRMED RUMORS:

Extraterrestrial craft are operating from underwater bases.

Advanced US sub-orbital weapons platforms represented as "tested" have actually been deployed from Vandenburg Air Force Base. These are armed with energy weapons.

UFO tracking has been moved from conventional to nanotechnology with microscopic sensors being used to detect behaviors, such as dimensional rifts and distortions in time things only discussed on TV shows like Fringe and X Files. (All Fox, oddly enough)

The actual classified memo on extremely short distribution mentions only the following:

Opposition is extraterrestrial and extremely aggressive and unfriendly

The threat represents a "clear and present danger" and is isolated to the Pacific Basin

China is forced to carry US responsibility because our own naval capability is sitting in the

Persian Gulf when America is under a exceedingly real threat.

Attempts to seek confirmations or to directly verify these operations will lead to fatal consequences.

What are the chances that we alone are the only inhabited planet among the trillions of other planets revolving around the hundreds of billions of Suns, within the millions of galaxies within this endless and constantly growing Universe? With all man's technology today, we cannot even figure out how to get out of our tiny solar system. Ever question why NASA did not build a space station on the moon? After all it is a solid mass, stationary, close to earth, may have water and we have Landed on it several times in the 60's and early 70's. Is it possible something prohibited us from doing so? Some say that astronaut's reported structures on the dark side of the moon made by others. Of course, we the common people would never know, but I'll bet there are many NASA people who do know. I heard a story once a long time ago that the astronauts were told by beings not from earth not to come back to the moon. Other stories say they saw something that scared them away.

Recently in 2011 and today the internet and youtube.com are filled with videos of craft coming and going from the surface of the moon. Not ours. There are even videos and stories about the US bombing parts of the moon. What for I wonder? It is without question that we common folk have no idea what our government is doing when it comes to space and UFOs, except for what they want to tell us.

Back to the science and Bible challenges, the Bible has many references to space and even stories of man leaving earth to go in space. Enoch was taken up into the heavens to meet God, and he was taught the ways and knowledge of his teachers. He then came back to earth. We are reading in the holy text that a living breathing person was taken to heaven and returned with knowledge that was so far advanced for his time and he lived to tell about it back on earth. He did not go in the spirit. He went as human flesh into a non-oxygen space that is as cold as hydrogen in the upper atmosphere of space, came back and lived to tell his story. How could this have been done in his time? Perhaps a spaceship of sort whisks him to heaven where he meets God and his angels?

Well if one assumes this fact to be true in the Bible, one has no alternative but to surmise this had to be a flying craft of some sort which took Enoch, Moses, Mohammed and, perhaps, Jesus when he spent forty days in the desert with nothing to eat or drink, somewhere in space itself, to a heaven which is not upon this earth. It had to have happened several times in the Bible as each was a different time in the stories told. Somehow we read the Bible and do not ponder on the statement it is saying to us pertaining to objects moving above and humans leaving earthly bounds, yet it has been in the Bible for thousands of years staring us in the face.

The Bible speaks of spacecraft however, they did not call them UFO's, they were called chariots of fire, shields, winged items of the sort.

Science cannot challenge this because they have no possible way to prove it ever existed. But the Bible says it did happen.

The next one that comes to mind is the plagues put upon the Pharaoh of Egypt in order to allow Moses to free the Jewish people out of bondage so they could return to Israel. Here scientists can give some reasonable explanation as to how this could happen, and to some extent, it is possible. According to some scientists it all started with the eruption of a volcano in another part of the world and if you follow the time line, it does make sense.

The plagues happened at the same time as a massive volcano eruption. The volcano Santorini [27] sent ash into the air affecting the surrounding area. The ash is found in Cairo and the Nile River, proven by testing the composition of the ash. This volcanic eruption happened between 1500-1650BC while the plagues happened between 1500-1550BC, so it fits.

> 1st plague. River ran red like blood. But there is a common algae plume called the red tide. This makes the river or any water, look red like blood. Why did this happen? The ash changes the PH level of the river allowing the algae to bloom.

> 2nd plague. Frogs. The algae is killing fish. Fish eat frog eggs. No fish, record number of frogs. Frogs cannot live in polluted water and so leave the river.

> 3rd and 4th plague. Lice and flies. The translation can actually be lice, fleas, gnats or midges. But you have river full of dead fish and now dead frogs. This brings the insects of the 3rd and 4th Plague.

---

27   One of the largest volcanic eruptions in recorded history: the Minoan eruption (sometimes called the **Thera eruption**), which occurred some 3600 years ago at the height of the Minoan civilization.

5th plague. Pestilence. flies, dead frogs, dead fish.

6th plague. Boils. Certain types of flies that bite can leave behind boils. The bites get infected, they turn in to boils.

7th plague. Fire and hail. Ash in the air causes a mixture of ash and water. The ash very high in the air causes the water to freeze so when it falls, it is hail and not rain. The fire was red lightning. It was red due to a chemical in the ash makes red lightning. So fire in the sky and hail.

8th plague. Locusts. locusts come about when the ground is particularly damp. They bury their eggs in the sand about 4-6 inches. After record amount of hail, the ground would be exceptionally wet allowing the locusts to form.

9th plague. Darkness. Ash in the air blocked the Sun light for days.

10th plague. Death of first born. In Egypt the first born would be the one to lead the family after the father died. When food was scarce the first born ate first and some time was the only one to eat. After locusts ate everything there was only grain locked in underground vaults. The hail got it wet, locust feces made it moldy, and so when only the first born ate they were the only ones killed by moldy grain. Granted that does not explain why the first sons of the Jews did not die but perhaps some did, but not as many as the Egyptian sons including the Pharaoh's.

So the real question is, how did God make the volcano erupt and tell Mosses these plagues would happen in that order? Was it God or the Elohim (those that came from above) who knew of the climatic changes that would take place and the causes? Mosses never saw God; he only heard his voice telling him what to do. The above chapter only points out an exceptionally small example of the science challenging the Bible's accuracy as to whether it is true to scripture. The fact so far is, the Bible is winning the battle in most of its stories as told in the days of old. Archeologists have confirmed Sodom and Gomorra did exist. They have noticed parts of the sand were turned to glass by what can only be explained as extremely high temperatures to cause fusion of this sort. It also had high levels of radiation. Someday soon the proof of the most famous of all, the Golden Ark of the Covenant will be displayed to mankind and then scientists around the globe will have the challenge of their lives. Do they dare open it or even touch it? My personal belief is, it has been stored in Ethiopia under lock and key by the Christian priests who have been guarding it for thousands of years. It is said that all of the guardian priest have lost most of their vision by just being close to it and many have died while in its custody.

The book of Exodus gives detailed instructions on how the Ark is to be constructed. It is to be 2½ cubits in length, 1½ in breadth and 1½ in height (as $21/2 \times 11/2 \times 11/2$ royal cubits or $1.31 \times 0.79 \times 0.79$ m, or $4.29 \times 2.59 \times 2.59$ feet). It is plated entirely with gold and a crown or molding of gold is put around it. Four rings of gold are to be attached to its four feet—two on each side—and through these rings staves of shittim-wood overlaid with gold for carrying the Ark are inserted and these are not to be removed. A golden cover adorned with golden cherubim is to be placed above the Ark.

Ethiopia, following its establishment in 1270, narrates how the real Ark of the Covenant was brought to Ethiopia by Menelik I with divine assistance while a forgery was left in the temple in Jerusalem. Although the *Kebra Nagast* is the best-known account of this belief, the belief predates the document. Abu Salih the Armenian, writing in the last quarter of the twelfth century, makes one early reference to this belief that they possessed the Ark. "The Abyssinians possess also the Ark of the Covenant", he wrote, and after a description of the object, describes how the liturgy is celebrated upon the Ark four times a year, "on the feast of the great nativity, on the feast of the glorious Baptism, on the feast of the holy Resurrection, and on the feast of the illuminating Cross. On 25 June 2009, the patriarch of the Orthodox Church of Ethiopia, Abune Paulos, said he would announce to the world the next day the unveiling of the Ark of the Covenant, which he said had been kept safe and secure in a church in Axum, Ethiopia. The following day, on 26 June 2009, the patriarch announced that he would not unveil the Ark after all, but instead he could attest to its current status

The biblical account relates that during the Israelites' exodus from Egypt, the Ark was carried by the priests some 2,000 cubits in advance of the people and their army or host. When the Ark was carried by priests into the bed of the Jordan, water in the river separated, opening a pathway for the entire host to pass through (Josh. 3:15-16; 4:7-18). The city of Jericho was taken with no more than a shout after the Ark of the Covenant was marched for seven days around it's wall by seven priests sounding seven trumpets of rams' horns (Josh. 6:4-20). When carried, the Ark was always wrapped in a veil, in skins and a blue cloth and was carefully concealed, even from the eyes of the priests who carried it. Why was the Ark so powerful? How can one communicate directly with God through it? Now that would be the most extraordinary scientific puzzle of all time to solve.

Note: The Bible tells us that Moses and the Israelites left Egypt and were in the desert for forty years. During this time they ate manna, we have no idea what manna was. They worshiped a bull made of gold. Moses was on the mountain for forty days with God, and when he returned he condemned them for idol worship. He had them build the Ark from the gold to house the commandments. They then followed an object of some sort which was in the sky and led them by day with smoke and fire by night. After countless possible explanations, one must conclude that whatever this object was, it stayed with them and was in the sky. I believe the ark was a communicator with not only their God, but it also had something to do with the object in the sky that was leading them to the land of milk and honey. It is said that when the object stopped and landed the people stopped and camped until the object returned to the sky above them and started to move again. Something about the Ark without a doubt must have been communicating with entities far superior than man. This is one of many cases where an object was in the sky as stated in the Bible and people witnessed a miracle of sort. Not knowing what it was, they called it what they best knew it to be based on their understanding at the time, hence we see the description of a shield, chariot, flying metal bird or any of the many statements in ancient text.

A perfect example is Jonah who appears in 2 Kings as a prophet. Jonah is miraculously saved after falling out of a boat during a storm by being swallowed by a large fish specially prepared by God, where he spends three days and three nights. In chapter two, while in the great fish, Jonah prays to God in his affliction and commits to thanksgiving and to paying what he has vowed. God commands the fish to spew Jonah out. The question here is, was it a fish, whale or something very different that held Jonah and misunderstood by the writers? Jonah could not have survived under those conditions and would have either drowned or been digested. Is it possible it may have been something that looked and acted like a fish? Something they saw, and were not able to identify except as a giant fish? What did the writers mean by "specially prepared by God"?

CHAPTER 6

One and Only GOD

Now that you have a better understanding of man's ancient history, it will be easier to understand the difference between God and the gods.

The Bible says that God is everywhere at all times and he sees all. In 2012 that is almost seven billion humans living here on earth. If there are others living on some other planet out there, he is seeing them too. After all God made everything in the entire Universe as stated in the Bible, so it all belongs to him. Right? Some of most fundamental questions asked for eons are who is, what is, and where is God? In reality, the three questions may be the same question asked three different ways. During the writing of this book, which has taken me much longer than I thought, I started reading a book recommended by a dear friend, and it helped me understand. Yes, even ministers still have questions about God. The book was written by a Tibetan monk who lived in the US and was on the verge of committing suicide when something extraordinarily strange happened to him that literally changed his life in a split second.

The name of the book is "The Children of the Law of One and the lost teaching of Atlantis." Now before you start thinking Atlantis, know this, scholars no longer dispute the existence of Atlantis.

They merely cannot agree on its location or its inhabitants. The book speaks of very old scriptures, and teachings of the monks who supposedly possess such writings. The Greeks believed in many gods, and according to Plato, Poseidon was the ruler of the Atlantic region and ruler of Atlantis. However, there has been no proof of such scriptures or ancient books presented for review, whereas the Sumerian tablets have been acknowledged. The monastery Jon Peniel trained at was so old, no one even knows who built it. The monks said it was built by the gods in the beginning of time. The book was written by Jon Peniel. It is about Tibetan monk beliefs. Our soul or spirit, which is our internal essence, our electrical field which is in and around us until the day we die, is set free to the Universe in another dimension. Jon's book chronicles his personal experiences and presents ancient spiritual teachings and philosophy. In order to make it as compelling and readable as possible, much of it is presented in a story and "dialogue" style based upon the author's experiences and conversations with monks, teachers and students.

Jon believed that it's best for everyone to attain a direct personal experience of God and discover the true nature of the Universe and creation for themselves, rather than taking anyone's word for it, or believing what they are told or read, and the teachings they provide such as "ancient history" concepts. The teachings provide the means for achieving that direct experience and direct "knowing" yourself. By reading the conversations and thoughts of the author as he is learning himself, you too can discover a return path to the Universal Spirit/God and inner peace. Western society calls it enlightenment. Hindus call it Nirvana.

Now I should inform the reader, I have read Jon's book for additional research into the writing of this book. However, after correlating the timelines, I find myself in a quandary. The Atlantian's came way after the creation of man according to some of the Greek text I have read. Plato tells of Atlantis and he was a man, first described by the ancient Greek historian Plato in 360 B.C. The mythological island was supposedly a formidable naval power before sinking into the sea over 10,000 years ago in a catastrophic event. Based on this story from Plato and others, I am more inclined to agree that the concept of the inner soul and enlightenment are more of the teachings of Buddhist Monks and their religious beliefs. However, I disagree with Jon's teachings of the soul coming to earth the way he describes it in his book. I agree that we humans have a soul and it resonates at a different frequency than the human body does, and when one dies, it is released to the Universal God and becomes part of the akashic records.

I do believe in Jesus Christ and his teachings as well as the miracles he performed here on earth. But for now the question and nature of the true GOD shall be discussed in this chapter.

We have all heard of the Big Bang theory and in the Cern project[28], scientists are trying to produce the God particle theory by smashing atom particles at light speed to see what becomes of them, as well as the elements it produces. Well, it seems that out of nothing, if left for billions of years, something happens. That is, nothing over time changes to something. Let's use bread as an example. Leave bread out and over time, mold forms which eats the bread and penicillin is formed. A crude form or explanation, but you get the picture.

The big bang was something like that, except in this case what was formed was pure energy. Something from nothing. The book of Genesis says: (Note: with authors remarks included)

- In the beginning, God created the heavens and the earth. Now the earth was formless and empty, darkness was over the surface of the deep and the Spirit of God was

---

28   CERN's main function is to provide the particle accelerators and other infrastructure needed for high-energy physics research

hovering over the waters. The question here is? Where did God come from, if in the beginning there was nothing? God was the pure energy (the spark), the something from nothing over time and space. The elusive Big Bang that science has been trying to find.

- God said, "Let there be light," and there was light. God saw that the light was good and he separated the light from the darkness. 5 God called the light "day," and the darkness he called "night." and there was evening and there was morning—the first day.

Here, we can see that when God made the heavens from himself, the pure energy, what he actually made were billions of galaxies and within each galaxy, billions of suns. The light was separated by light years within the vast darkness of space, all a part of God and energy.

- God said, "Let there be a vault between the waters to separate water from water." So God made the vault and separated the water under the vault from the water above it. And it was so. God called the vault "sky." and there was evening and there was morning—the second day. This may mean the ice and water particles within the frozen space, such as comets made of ice or as we humans call H2O. A mixture of hydrogen and oxygen.

Space is more than 80 % hydrogen, it is our suns fuel. It is the most abundant chemical in the entire Universe.

- God said, "Let the water under the sky be gathered to one place and let dry ground appear." and it was so. God called the dry ground "land," and the gathered waters he called "seas." and God saw that it was good. No need to explain, but note the land was immensely different back then if you consider the plate movements over millions of years here on earth. In fact, they are still moving like wax on water. Ever so slowly, but forever moving.

• Then God said, "Let the land produce vegetation: seed-bearing plants and trees on the land that bear fruit with seed in it, according to their various kinds." and it was so. The land produced vegetation: plants bearing seed according to their kinds and trees bearing fruit with seed in it according to their kinds. God saw that it was good. And there was evening and there was morning—the third day.

• God said, "Let there be lights in the vault of the sky to separate the day from the night and let them serve as signs to mark sacred times and days and years, and let them be lights in the vault of the sky to give light on the earth." and it was so. God made two great lights—the greater light to govern the day and the lesser light to govern the night. He also made the stars. God set them in the vault of the sky to give light on the earth, to govern the day and the night and to separate light from darkness. God saw that it was good. And there was evening and there was morning—the fourth day.

• God said, "Let the water teem with living creatures and let birds fly above the earth across the vault of the sky." So God created the great creatures of the sea and every living thing with which the water teems and that moves about in it, according to their kinds and every winged bird according to its kind. God saw that it was good. God blessed them and said, "Be fruitful and increase in number and fill the water in the seas and let the birds increase on the earth." and there was evening and there was morning—the fifth day.

- God said, "Let the land produce living creatures according to their kinds: the livestock, the creatures that move along the ground and the wild animals, each according to its kind." and it was so. God made the wild animals according to their kinds, the livestock according to their kinds and all the creatures that move along the ground according to their kinds. God saw that it was good.

- Then God said, "**Let us make mankind in our image**, in our likeness, so that they may rule over the fish in the sea and the birds in the sky, over the livestock and all the wild animals and over all the creatures that move along the ground."

Notice this is plural, meaning more than one. If God was alone when he was to make man, why is the statement from the Bible plural? "*Let us*" "*our likeness*"? Many parts of the Bible were rewritten using the Torah and Sumerian tablets as a guide which the writer's had read, which in this case would be the Elohim or Anunnaki as Gods making man in their image. If that was the intent while writing the Bible, it makes logical sense if we read the Genesis making of man from the perspective of a higher being, in this case, it may have been the Sumerian gods, the Anunnaki.

- So God created mankind in his own image, in the image of God he created them;   male and female he created them.

- God blessed them and said to them, "Be fruitful and increase in number; fill the earth and subdue it. Rule over the fish in the sea and the birds in the sky and over every living creature that moves on the ground."

- Then God said, "I give you every seed-bearing plant on the face of the whole earth and every tree that has fruit with seed in it. They will be yours for food. And to all the beasts of the earth and all the birds in the sky and all the creatures that move along the ground—everything that has the breath of life in it—I give every green plant for food." and it was so.

- God saw all that he had made and it was very good. And there was evening and there was morning—the sixth day.

The entire creation in Genesis says it all happened in 6 days. What were 6 days according to God? Back then was time the same as it is now? My position on the Genesis scripture is decidedly different, so I will attempt to explain.

Every story has to start somewhere and end. The creation story is no different, but when you think about it and compare it to the scientific study, everything is slightly out of reality within time as it is written in Genesis.

Here is how I believe creation started.

THE ONE TRUE GOD

God was the Big Bang, the pure energy that started everything within the universe as we know it. His essence and spirit was in everything because it was all a part of him and therefore him, as the universal spirit or essence or energy. However you choose to call it, it was all part of God. We know that earth was remarkably different when it was formed. Even before the prehistoric age, the earth had to cool down, create oxygen and so many other things had to happen before man or animals would have been able to came into existence and survive on the primitive earth. That is absolute fact! Nothing could live on earth until plants produced enough oxygen in the atmosphere for any living walking, flying creature could survive. It is scientifically known that the oxygen levels back in prehistoric times were higher than they are now. That would mean that plants, trees and all living green life had to grow first and take hundreds if not thousands of years to change the atmosphere to breathable oxygen levels.

As stated in prior chapters, our Sun is older than the earth by billions of years, somewhere around six to seven billion years old, our earth is between three -four billion years old. Planets within our tiny solar system are of various ages. With that said, how can it even be possible to create everything in six days? Common sense tells us, the timing does not add up. From a scientific position let us remove the entire genesis hypostasis of creation of the Universe and start Genesis with the making of man. Instead of God of the Bible, let us substitute the Anunnaki gods who made man. Now it makes undeniable sense that the genesis theory could have happened in this way and the writers of the Bible had a need to explain the beginning of time, where the stars and sky came from in an effort to a beginning. The writers may have tied two gods together without even knowing it. The God (big bang energy God) of the Universe and the Sumerian gods. God was not limited to earthly forms of life and could have produced many other forms of life within the universe.

I am 100 percent convinced that the one true God is a Universal God. The universe and everything in it is God. We are a part of the planet earth and therefore, part of God. Our soul is the energy part of God, which never dies and goes on forever. When Jesus said we could live in eternity with God, he was surely speaking of our soul and spirit and definitely not our body.

Our body is merely the vessel which a soul chooses to occupy in an effort to learn and experience what we as humans take for granted every day of our living life, touch, feel, love, sorrow, pain, excitement, joy, pleasure and most powerful of all learning and knowledge.

You see, I believe our soul's purpose is to learn what it cannot experience as a soul and spirit because it is not human, it is pure energy. As pure energy, it can travel at the speed of light. And it must harbor memory because there are thousands of stories of people being someone else or somewhere else in time. It therefore must be a resident of the human brain. When someone dies it is always said from those who have come back from the dead who claim to have seen family, and friends who had died, and they were somewhere else in time. No one in the thousands of near death experience has ever returned to report entry into nothingness! To them it was heaven, enlightenment, nirvana, warmth, love, peaceful pure energy that carried with it memory and knowledge.

The soul and spirit in all of us maintains the entire life memory of our human existence it had within us, while alive on earth.

Many have written books about this subject and according to Carl Sagan "We are all made of star stuff". We are all a part of the akashic[29] records. Akasha is a Sanskrit word meaning "sky", "space" or "aether" and is described as containing all knowledge of human experience and all experiences as well as the history of the cosmos encoded or written in the very aether or fabric of all existence. The records or The Book of Life in the Bible (Psalm 69:28, Philippians 4:3, Revelation 3:5, 13:8, 17:8, 20:12, 20:15 and Revelation 21:27) are metaphorically on a non-physical plane described as a library; other analogies commonly found in discourse on the subject include a "universal supercomputer" and the "Mind of God." People who describe the records assert that they are constantly updated

---

29   The akashic records, -word meaning "sky", "space" and is described as containing all knowledge of human experience and all experiences.

automatically and that they can be accessed through astral projection or under deep hypnosis. The most famous user of this concept was the remarkable Edgar Casey, who used the records for hundreds of hypnotically induced trances he had during his readings. Throughout history, many have been able to tap into these records. Nostradamus claimed to have gained access. The Bible refers to the Akasha records as the Book of Life in both the Old Testament (Psalm 69:28) and the New Testament (Philippians 4:3, Revelation 3:5, 13:8, 17:8, 20:12, 20:15 and Revelation 21:27.

I remember a story of a little boy who at the age of 3 told his family he was a pilot in the Second World War, and he flew a certain type of plane. James' parents say he revealed extraordinary details about the life of a former fighter pilot. They say he told them his plane had been hit by the Japanese and crashed. James told his father he flew a Corsair. James also told his father the name of the boat he took off from was the Natoma, and the name of someone he flew with was Jack Larson. After some research, His father Bruce discovered both the Natoma and Jack Larson were real. The Natoma Bay was a small aircraft carrier in the Pacific. James had also begun signing his crayon drawings "James 3." Bruce soon learned that the only pilot from the squadron killed at Iwo Jima was James M. Huston Jr. James was able to recognize one of Huston's former shipmates after 60 years. "His comment was, 'They're all so old.'". His mother served meatloaf one night for dinner, and her son never had it before "When he sat down, he said, 'Meatloaf! I have not had that since I was on the Natoma.

The father found that a family relative was still alive; I think it may have been a sister. The boy and she met and she showed the boy pictures and the boy cried uncontrollably with memories of his souls past life. The sister was so convinced that this little boy was the reincarnation of her brother, she gave him her brother's medals and picture. The boy's family decided to help release the inner soul of the pilot for the sake of the child being normal again.

They chartered a fishing boat off Japan, and the boy spoke to his inner soul and told him to follow the light, he had to let him go. Reluctantly the boy laid flowers at the spot where the pilot went down and cried uncontrollably while saying goodbye. James' vivid alleged recollections are starting to fade as he gets older. Today he is in his 20s. It is common for most children who have imaginary friends or talk about things misunderstood by adults. Their souls are pure and have not been rooted in human experience like older children. Meaning, the more children learn from their surroundings and people, the more rooted the body is to being human, and the soul is secondary in thought. As the boy got older he slowly forgot the soldier soul within and returned to a normal young boy growing up. He still loves planes of the type his soul once flew in the war.

A point made here is, all children have pure and uncorrupted minds, and their souls are on the surface interacting with the child. Imaginary friends only they can see. Talking to dead family members and holding conversations with what we may think is no one. Scary to most, but perfectly normal to others, who understand the concept of the soul, life, after death and reincarnation.

My own grandson was talking to my dead mother one week after she died. When I asked him what he was looking at, he said "He was talking to grandma in the cloud." A moment in my life and those who were there will never forget. Of course, I cried uncontrollably. However my grandson told me "Don't cry, grandma is ok, she is happy."

I will share my own experience with seeing something strange and incomprehensible to me at the time. I saw my mother's soul in my backyard the moment she died. It was extremely quick, and it was a ghostly silhouette of a woman in white, floating at the edge of my fence by the pool. It lasted only two seconds, and then the phone rang. It was my father telling me my mother had just passed away. I knew deep inside me that my mother just died and had a yearning feeling when I saw the ghostly figure, like our souls were acknowledging each other for those brief moments. I remember it like it was yesterday. I will never forget how my soul felt the connection, all before the call, confirming her death. My father and my brother died a year later from broken hearts. My parents were married over fifty years. It was a tough time in my life back then. Many of you have heard stories from others or had some type of apparition. It must be another dimension that is not of this world we live in. Perhaps another dimensions that physicists speak of, or as I call it, "The spiritual world where we go to a higher dimension". I would do anything to see them again for ten seconds. Anything!

Another story is that of General George Patton:

George Patton believed in reincarnation. He remembered fighting the Romans as Hannibal of Carthage and his Carthaginian army. Patton studied Rommel's book and tactics to defeat his Panzer battalion in North Africa. Patton also believed he was with Napoleon in battles. Hannibal's foe, Rome was ultimately defeated by Germanic tribes. Patton beat the Germans. They both died a strange death. Although each undoubtedly had a strong ego, their men would follow them anywhere. While in France, he said, "I know it well." Patton felt sure that he had been to France before in a previous life, he pointed out the sites of the ancient Roman temples and amphitheater, the drill ground and the forum, even showing a spot where Julius Caesar had made his camp. Patton later told his nephew, "It is as if someone were at my ear whispering the directions"

I am sure; there are thousands of documented cases of the afterlife and past lives. A great saying from the movie Ghost, "Molly, you take it all with you on the other side". Every one of us has had some unexplainable experience in our life, or knows of someone who has.

I have had many things happen to me that I could not explain, but I remember them like it was yesterday.

Now, examining the Sumerian scripts and what they scribed about creation;

- They are different, yet eerily similar to the Bible, keeping in mind, the Bible is selective and was written using the Jewish Torah, and stories they passed down from generation to generation, always changing through interpretation of the original story.

- One must ask the inevitable question "Is it possible that the God of the Bible is that of the Sumerian gods, and the God who made the Universe and everything in it is a Universal God"? A Universal God who sees all at the same time and is everywhere? An all knowing God by use of the Akashic records, the fabric energy of the Universe.

- When pondered upon in this perspective, the Bible makes complete sense when it states that God sees everything and knows all.

- To me, it allows me to distinguish between the Bible God and the spiritual God of the Universe.

The Epic of Creation is the Sumerian version of how the world of man began and includes to some degree the formation of the other members of the solar system. The Sumerian tale may likely be the source of the earliest chapters of the Bibles' Genesis, the fact that the Torah was written during the Hebrews' captivity in Babylon around 600 B.C.E. and the Sumerian stories were written thousands of years earlier and past down from generation to generation. The Sumerian Epic of Creation and Genesis both have an interesting feature of being scientifically accurate in terms of what was created first. All of the other planets may be considered to have been described in various stages of grouping themselves into the current arrangement according to the Sumerian epic. However, the bible does not go into detail about planet formation whereas the Sumerian scripts do expand on this topic.

The case of the planets being named is well presented by Zecharia Sitchin in his book, *The 12th Planet*. Sitchin makes it clear that the planetary description aspect of the Epic is justified and that the planets and gods were closely linked. This is extremely crucial in the Sumerian version of creation and probably why the Genesis version is shorter. One assumes, for example, that the Hebrew writers of Genesis (circa 600 B.C.E.) would not want multiple gods in their story furthermore; they would not want to limit its supreme deity to any one celestial body. Cut all the allusions to planets and you don't have as much to write about. There was also undoubtedly a strong inclination not to add anything to the creation story and keep it uncomplicated.

BASED ON THE COSMIC CODE:
THE SIXTH BOOK OF THE EARTH CHRONICLES
BY ZECHARIA SITCHIN:

Written with permission, file on record.

Zecharia Sitchin wrote in his book that the Sumerian text talked about and documented their celestial gods. Some seven thousand clay tablets recorded everything from marriages to wars. According to some of these tablets, the following emerges:

- Around 400,000 years ago a group of human-like beings called the Anunnaki, came to earth in search of gold. Their planet was called Nibiru. The discovery of gold could be used to protect their planet's atmosphere.

- Led by Enki the Anunnaki landed on earth near the waters of the Persian Gulf.

- Around 330,000, which was 70,000 years later, more Anunnaki arrive on earth, among them Enki's half-sister who was a medical official.

- As gold production faltered near the Persian Gulf it was decided to mine additional gold out of Africa.

- Seven functional settlements in southern Mesopotamia were built. The refined gold is stored and sent to orbiters.

- 2500,000 (50,000 years later)

The Anunnaki toiling in the gold mines mutinied over the hard labor and it was decided that they create primitive workers through genetic manipulation of Ape woman which were found on earth in the African region. Primitive man took over the manual chores of the Anunnaki. Enlil who was originally the leader brought the primitive workers to the Edin in Mesopotamia. Given the ability to procreate, Homo sapiens began to multiply.

Note: This may be the creation of Adam as stated in the Bible. The Bible was written well after 600 BCE by people who were leaving this area and took with them the creation story. To the humans, Enlil was their god, and that may be where we get the individualization of a one God as in the Bible story. Based on understanding, it was one God who took credit for the creation of man as stated in one of the seven tablets of Sumerian text. It coincides with the seventh day of rest in the Bible, and the seventh day of praise to Enlil in Sumerian tablet.

- 100,000

  Climate warmed again. Other Anunnaki arrived on earth and found the daughters of man to be fair, (the biblical Nephilim) to Enlil's growing annoyance, marry the daughters of man and bare children, located in Genesis six. In fact the Bible mentions giants eight times.

- 49,000

  Enki and Ninhursag elevated humans of Anunnaki parentage to rule over mankind. These rulers were known as demigods.

- Sometime around 13,000

  Realizing that Nibiru in earth's proximity would trigger havoc on earth, Enlil made the Anunnaki swear to keep the impending calamity a secret from mankind.

- 11,000 B.C.

  Enki broke the oath, and instructed Noah to build a ship. The Deluge swept over the earth.

- Enlil agreed to grant the remnants of mankind implements and seeds. Agriculture began in the highlands.

- From the timeline stated in prior chapters, the Bible scholars say the great flood happened in 2348 BC. The Sumerian tablets state that sometime around 11,000 BC Noah was instructed to build a boat. If the bible account is correct, then the pyramids were built after the flood, and Edgar Casey may have been correct in predicting the pyramid building was around 10,500 BC. The Bible mentions nothing about the greatest manmade achievement in history, either in the Old Testament or the New Testament.

It is not stated in the Sumerian tablets that Noah was to collect animals at the time however; somehow the animals did survive the flood as stated in the Bible. It may be possible that if the Anunnaki were performing genetic engineering on Homo sapiens at the time, it may also be possible the Anunnaki stored the DNA of animals to reintroduce back to earth after the flood. Some researchers state that the flood may have been isolated to the Sinai region, which would make more sense than the entire earth being flooded; leaving many species of animals alive during this event and only the animals of the region were lost to the flood event.

- 10,500 B.C.

  The descendants of Noah were allotted three regions. The Sinai Peninsula was retained by the Anunnaki and a control center was established on Mount Moriah (the future Jerusalem).

- The poem of Ur to Enlil is as follows: Enlil's commands are by far the loftiest, his words are holy, his utterances are immutable! The fate he decides is everlasting; his glance makes the mountains anxious, his voice reaches into the interior of the mountains. All the gods of the earth bow down to father Enlil, who sits comfortably on the holy dais, the lofty engur, to Nunamnir, whose lordship and princeship are most perfect. The Annanuki entered before him and obeyed his instructions faithfully.

- 9,780 B.C.

  Ra/Marduk, Enki's firstborn son, divided dominion over

Egypt between Osiris and Seth. This was the worship of the Sun God Ra at the same time.

- Seth seized and dismembered Osiris and assumed sole rule over the Nile Valley.

- 8,670 B.C.

  The victorious Ninurta emptied the Great Pyramid of its equipment.

Recent speculation contends that the great pyramids of Egypt may have been some sort of energy generator. There are pictorials of a sort of bulb being lit by a machine or perhaps the Bagdad batteries. No bodies were ever found in either of the great pyramids.

- The division of Earth was reaffirmed. Rule over Egypt transferred from the Ra/Marduk dynasty to that of Thoth, who built Baalbek as a substitute Beacon City later called Heliopolis by Alexander the great after he gained control. The ruins are one of the most extraordinary and enigmatic holy places of ancient times. Long before the Romans, even before the Phoenicians constructed a temple to the god Baal, there stood at Baalbek the largest stone block construction found in the entire world. The Romans who called it the house of Jupiter were the last to build at the site.

- 8,500 B.C.

  The Anunnaki established outposts at the gateway to the space facilities. Jerusalem was one of them. This was where King Solomon was instructed to build the temple of God and is still known as the temple mount today.

- As the era of peace continued, the Anunnaki granted

mankind new advances. The Neolithic period begins. Demi-gods rule over Egypt. All ruling pharaoh's were known to be demi-gods and were in communication with their gods through their high priests.

- Marduk proclaimed Babylon "Gateway of the Gods." The (Tower of Babel incident.) The Anunnaki decide to confuse mankind's languages. Marduk/Ra returned to Egypt and deposed Thoth to take back the leadership of the region.

- 3, 350 - 3,100

  250 years of chaos ended with the installation of an Egyptian Pharaoh in Memphis.

- 2,123 B.C Abraham of the Bible was born in Nippur.

- 2,113 A Nippurian priest-Terah, Abraham's father, came to Ur to liaison with its royal court.

- 2,048

  Abraham was ordered to southern Canaan with an elite corps of cavalrymen.

- Amar-Sin (the biblical Amraphel) became king of Ur. Abraham went to Egypt, stayed five years and then returned to Ur with more troops.

Around 2,024 BC, Marduk returned to Babylon. The Anunnaki council approved the use of nuclear weapons on the spaceport in Jerusalem. Some proof remains within Jerusalem because of high radiation levels around the region. Nergal and Ninurta destroyed the Spaceport and the errant Canaanite cities. This may be the location of the story of destruction of Sodom and Gomorrah, as well as some ancient cities in India. Proof of a horrific intense fire does exist within these recently found cities. Fused rocks and silica glass lay credence to the effects of nuclear results. The winds carried the radioactive cloud to Sumer which is modern day Iraq. People died, the soil became a barren desert. Sumer and its magnificent civilization lie prostrate. Its legacy passed to Abraham's seed at the age of 100, a legitimate heir Isaac.

Abraham[30] is mentioned nine times in the Sumerian clay tablets. This is the same Abraham in the Bible. The difference is the Sumerian depiction is much more detail than the Bible account. There are many similarities between the timeline of the Sumerian text and the Bible. Some of the names are different however; the stories are extraordinarily similar in both. In the lineage from Noah to Abraham the two most powerful men are Shem, Noah's son who was the Great High Priest and Shem's great-grandson Eber.

As noted in the Bible:

Genesis: 22:9

- Abraham built an altar there and arranged the wood on it. He bound his son Isaac and laid him on the altar, on top of the wood. Then he reached out his hand and took the knife to slay his son. But the angel of the Lord called out to him from heaven, "Abraham! Abraham!"

- "Here I am," he replied. "Do not lay a hand on the boy," he said. "Do not do anything to him. Now I know that you fear God because you have not withheld from me your son, your only son." The angel of the Lord called to Abraham from heaven a second time and said, "I swear by myself, declares the Lord, that because you have done

---

30   Abraham is the founding father of the Israelites, with a prominent role in Judaism, Christianity and Islam.

this and have not withheld your son, your only son, I will surely bless you and make your descendants as numerous as the stars in the sky and as the sand on the seashore. Your descendants will take possession of the cities of their enemies, and through your offspring, all nations on earth will be blessed because you have obeyed me."

Abraham never saw God; he heard him or the angels from heaven above? Think about this for a moment, God spoke to Abraham from heaven? Understanding , God is not a person and speaking is a Human thing, so could it be that this God was either an Anunnaki leaders speaking or the spirit of the universal God speaking to Abraham's soul? We will never know. We do know God has spoken many times in the Bible. The question is, was it God, or someone else that was a God in those days? If God is pure energy and is everywhere as the spirit of the entire universe, does he actually speak? Was this a test to see if Abraham was loyal and obedient to his tribal leader, or was his inner soul (spirit of God) telling him this information? We have no proof as the Bible says God spoke to people in the Bible and the clay tablets from the Sumerians speak of their gods living and speaking to them, the Anunnaki. Is it possible that if we read in the Bible that God speaks, it may have been the Elohim god and not the Universal God?

My personal concept of God and gods is, to try and make sense of the information we have at hand. The Bible some Three thousand years old, the thousands of clay tablets from the Sumerians, around six thousand years old and the hidden scripts in the Tibetan monastery as yet unknown of age or origin, all speak of a past we cannot be sure of, and scientists as well as archeologist around the world are trying to prove or disprove it, who or what should we believe.

Careful mathematical calculations led me to notice the timeline according to Zachariah Sitchin does not line up with the Bible time line. Although the creation of Adam is mentioned in the Bible it is in Sumerian tablets as well. Using the Bible, starting from Abraham and going back to Adam, a total of six thousand and seventeen years passed. Going back to the Sumerian tablets, it claims that mankind was engineered genetically around two hundred thousand years ago. Taking into account this was the earliest form of man it is still a far different timeline which puts Adam in the Bible creation far later in time. Although the timeline may be incorrect the stories of creation are quite remarkable in both renditions.

TIMELINE FROM ABRAHAM BACK TO ADAM, STARTING WITH ADAM ACCORDING TO THE BIBLE:

Biblical Timeline	Bible Reference	
4004 BC	Adam and Eve	Genesis 5:3-5
	Cain	Genesis 4:1, 17-22
	Abel	Genesis 4:2, 8-10
3874 BC	Seth	Genesis 5:6-7
3769 BC	Enos	Genesis 5:9-11
3679 BC	Cainan	Genesis 5:12-14
3609 BC	Mahalaleel	Genesis 5:15-17
3544 BC	Jared	Genesis 5:18-20
3382 BC	Enoch (walks with God)	Genesis 5:21-24
3317 BC	Methuselah (longest lived)	Genesis 5: 25-29

3004 BC - 2348 BC Noah to the Flood

3130 BC	Lamech	Genesis 5:28-31
3074 BC	Adam dies	Genesis 5:3-5
2948 BC	Noah	Gen 5:32, 9:18, 28, 29
2864 BC	Enos dies	Genesis 5: 9-11
2348 BC	The Flood	Genesis 7

2348 BC - 2004 BC the Flood to Abraham

2348 BC	the Flood	Genesis 7
2346 BC	Arpachshad	Genesis 11:12-13
2311 BC	Selah	Genesis 11:14-15
2281 BC	Eber	Genesis 11: 15-18
2247 BC	Peleg	Genesis 11: 18-19
2217 BC	Reu	Genesis 11: 20-21
2200 BC	Tower of Babel	Genesis 10:25
2185 BC	Serug	Genesis 11:22-23
2155 BC	Nahor	Genesis 11: 24-26
2136 BC	Terah	Genesis 11: 26-32
1996 BC	Abraham	Genesis 25:7-8

The major problem with the listed timeline is the fact that the Bible scholars claim that man is approximately six thousand years old. This is completely impossible as scientific proof and architectural proof exist which are dated much earlier than six thousand years. The Egyptian Pyramids were purportedly built about four–five thousand years ago. As noted from the biblical timeline, that would mean that Adam was created about two thousand years before the pyramids. If this is true then the pyramids had been built before the flood, tower of Babel and according to the Bible, the flood was 2348 BC. Estimates of the Pyramids using carbon dating put the time between 2889BC to 2503BC.

Somehow, the dates are wrong as there is no mention of the building of the Pyramids in the Bible. How is it possible, that one of the largest structures on earth was not included? Edgar Cayce, who was an early twentieth-century psychic claimed that the Sphinx and Khufu's Great Pyramid were built in 10,500 B.C. Archaeologists believe it is the work of the Old Kingdom Dynasty society that rose to prominence in the Nile Valley from 3000 B.C. and built the Giza Pyramids between 2889 and 2503 B.C. which according to the Bible timeline still means the Pyramids were built before the great flood.

I am inclined to believe Edgar Cayce was correct and the Pyramids are much older than Archaeologist claim. One cannot rule out the possibility that the Bible timeline may be wrong; however, it is yet to be challenged. Many archeologist claim the sphinx shows erosion by water which could validate the pyramids and sphinx were built before the flood and water damage was a result of the event. No matter how you move the dates, it is certain; the Pyramids had to be built before the great flood in 2348BC. If the Biblical dates are true, all mankind was wiped out, including Egypt and the Nephilim (giants) of that time period. If on the other hand, the Sumerian tablets are correct and Noah was instructed to build a boat in 11,000 BC, than the Pyramids would have been built before the great flood also.

Herodotus wrote of the Great Pyramid after visiting Egypt in about 450 BC and talked with the old priests there and heard their account of the construction of the pyramids. That was at least a thousand years after Pharaoh Cheops had built his pyramid sometime around 1450BC.

I find it ironic that science and archeologist cannot agree or pin down a precise date for any of the above accounts of history using all the technology available in the 21st century. Either way, it must be noted that all the dates of the Pyramids still put them before the great flood mentioned in the Bible. The Bible does mention the fact that an alter was to be built in the center of Egypt for the purpose of praising God however, it is a poor assumption that this entry was referring to the great Pyramids of Egypt. I have searched for any written account of the pyramids being in the Bible and found nothing of the sort.

CHAPTER 7

Show Me the Proof

What we do know and have concrete evidential proof of are well known sites around the world.

- **Ancient Maps :** In 1513, the Ottoman Turkish admiral Piri Reis drew a world map that has been said to show part of the Antarctic continent. Gregory McIntosh and other cartographers and historians who have examined the map in detail believe the resemblance of the coastline to the actual coast of Antarctica to be tenuous. For centuries before the actual discovery of Antarctica, cartographers had been depicting a massive southern landmass on global maps. Since the Antarctic continent was not officially sighted until 1820 and its full coastline was not known until much later; this claim, if true, would require substantial revisions to the history of exploration, settlement, evolution and technological advancements of the time.

- **Tiwanaku**: Is recognized by andean scholars as one of the most prominent precursors to the Inca Empire, flourishing as the ritual and administrative capital of a substantial state power for approximately five hundred years. In

1945, Arthur Posnansky estimated that Tiwanaku dated to 15,000 BC using archaeoastronomical techniques. Later, as a result of the reevaluation of the techniques that Posnansky used to estimate the age of Tiwanaku, expert archaeoastronomical archaeologists concluded that they were invalid as they were a "sorry example of misused archaeoastronomical evidence." The correct date may be between 10,000 and 12,000 BC. Stone slabs weighing more than 100 tons were bought seven to 15 miles up a mountain side 17,000 feet high and perfectly placed one on top another, with no mortar. They did find that each slab was connected by a piece of melted iron looking like the letter I that held the slabs together side by side. The same interlocking use was found in Egypt and Mexico structures. Primitive man did this? I don't think so!

- **Egypt pyramids** : were built using stones cut into many tons and we still do not know how they were actually built. In fact, we do not even know what they were actually used for since there were no mummies found in the famous pyramids themself. They all point to the Pleiades group of stars, specifically Orion's belt. Why? Its central claim is that there is a correlation between the location of the three largest pyramids of the Giza pyramid complex and the three middle stars of the constellation Orion, and that this correlation was intended as such by the builders of the pyramids. The stars of Orion were associated with Osiris, the sun-God of rebirth and afterlife, and rebirth by the ancient Egyptians. Orion was also identified with Unas, the last Pharaoh of the Fifth Dynasty, who was said to have eaten the flesh of his enemies and devoured the gods themselves to become dominant, and bring inheritance of his power. According to myth, Unas travels through the sky to become the star Sabu, or Orion. Because pharaohs were believed to be transformed into Osiris after death, some of the greatest pyramids – the ones at Giza – were built to mirror the pattern of the stars in the constellation. To make the transformation easier, the air shaft in the King's Chamber in the Great Pyramid was aligned with the star Alnitak, Zeta Orion's the easternmost star in Orion's Belt.

Note: The Egyptian pyramids are the most famous of all the pyramids, but did you know there are thousands of pyramids throughout the world less know such as The temple of Ur in Iraq, Peru has over Three hundred pyramids, Egypt has one hundred fifty five, two hundred in China, North Sudan, India, Mexico, South and North America all of similar design in structure The Mayans built more than any other and a small percentage have been found.

- **The Mayans** : Discoveries of Maya occupation at Cuello, Belize have been carbon dated to around 2600 BC, built pyramids half way around the world and they too point to the Pleiades' group. They formed a calendar more precise than ours. They introduced the number zero. They had more knowledge about the universe than anyone could possibly now and they were correct based on scientific study. Each of the four sides of the pyramid has its own stairway of 91 steps. The four sides share one step with the top platform. If you calculate the number of total steps (91 x 4 +1) you will arrive at the number 365 which is the number of days in one solar year. The ancient Mayans built these gargantuan structures without the help of domesticated animals or wheels, which had not been invented, or metal tools since they were not commonly used in the region they inhabited. The tools they had were extremely simple like basalt axes and fire axes used on wood while they used tools made of quartzite, limestone, granite, obsidian and flint on stone.

- **Concerning their 2012 prediction**The Mayan Calendar actually started with the Olmecs, not the Mayans. The Olmecs were given this calendar by their god Quetzalcoatl, the Mayans called him Kukulcan or Ququmatz, to the Ancient Egyptians he was known as Thoth. He was known by different names to different civilizations, but to the Sumerians he was known as Ningishzidda. Ningishzidda was one of the Anunnakis who came to Earth from Nibiru! According to ancient texts Quetzalcoatl/Ningishzidda, before he left, promised that he would return and his return would be at the end of a cycle (December 21,2012). In fact in 1519 the Aztecs mistook the Spanish conquistador Hernan Cortes as Quetzalcoatl. In 1519, when Cortes and his men showed up in what is now Veracruz, the natives greeted them with gifts thinking that it was the promised return of their God, not knowing that the Spaniards were there to take over their land, it ultimately led to the fall of the Aztec Empire. (The Fall of the Aztec Empire) So this is the real Mayan Prophecy - it's the return of their God, Quetzalcoatl.

So does this mean that the Anunnaki will come back to Earth in 2012? Not exactly, in the past, the Anunnaki comings and goings to and from our planet occurred when Nibiru was close to our planet and as you have read, Nibiru has a 3,600 year orbit, so that is approximately every 3,600 years. According to Zecharia Sitchin the date December 21, 2012 is wrong and only represents a new cycle of the calendar and the year should actually be 2087. Oddly enough, Sir Isaac Newton spent 25 years trying to decipher the Bible code and predicted the year to be 2160 based on the book of Daniel chapter 12.

- Mr. Sitchin claimed Isaac Newton used the Gregorian calendar, whereas Sitchin used the Sumerian calendar.

- **Baalbek** The history of settlement in the area of Baalbek dates back about 9,000 years, with almost continual settlement of the Temple of Jupiter above the previous structure, which was a temple since the pre-Hellenistic era. The Roman construction was built on top of earlier ruins and involved the creation of an immense raised plaza onto which the actual buildings were placed. The sloping terrain necessitated the creation of retaining walls on the north, south and west sides of the plaza. These walls are built of about 24 monoliths at their lowest level each weighing approximately 300 tons. The western, tallest retaining wall has a second course of monoliths containing the famous trilithon: a row of three stones, each over 19 metros long, 4.3 metros high and 3.6 meters broad, cut from limestone. They weigh approximately 800 tons each. A fourth, still larger stone called Stone of the Pregnant Woman lies unused in a nearby quarry about 1 mile from the town, it's weight, often exaggerated, is estimated at 1,000 tons. An even larger stone, weighing approximately 1,200 tons, lies in the same quarry across the road. Another of the Roman ruins, the Great Court, has six 20 m (65.62 Ft) tall stone columns surviving, out of an original 128 columns. No modern machine today could move these gigantic cut stone slabs.

- **Pumapunku Bolivia.** The Pumapunku is a terraced earthen mound that is faced with megalithic blocks. This terrace is paved with multiple enormous stone blocks.

The Platform contains the largest stone slab found in both the Pumapunku and Tiwanaku Site. This stone slab is 7.81 meters long, 5.17 meters wide and averages 1.07 meters thick. Based upon the specific gravity of the red sandstone from which it was carved, this stone slab has been estimated to weigh 131 metric tons. Current understanding of this complex is limited due to its age, the lack of a written record. Each stone was finely cut to interlock with the surrounding stones and the blocks fit together like a puzzle, forming load-bearing joints without the use of mortar. One common engineering technique involves cutting the top of the lower stone at a certain angle and placing another stone on top of it which was cut at the same angle The precision with which these angles have been utilized to create flush joints is indicative of a highly sophisticated knowledge of stone-cutting and a thorough understanding of descriptive geometry Many of the joints are so precise that not even a razor blade will fit between the stones. Much of the masonry is characterized by accurately cut rectilinear blocks of such uniformity that they could be interchanged for one another while maintaining a level surface and even joints. The blocks were so precisely cut as to suggest the possibility of prefabrication and mass production. No tools were ever found and the cuttings of the stone are perfect as a laser cutter with elaborate designs. This site is still being studied today and architects are baffled as to how this could have been done with nothing but handmade tools. In fact, they say "it is totally impossible". So much for a professional opinion.

- **Anasazi**: or "ancestral Puebloans," lived in a place called Chaco Canyon and the layout represents the stars above the site. Chaco people built the Great House as a lunar observatory precisely aligned to a celestial event that occurs just once in a generation.

- **The Hopi Indians**: say they communicate with the star brothers through their rituals and dances. An ancient Hopi Indian prophecy states, "When the Blue Star Kachina makes its appearance in the heavens, the Fifth World will emerge". This will be the Day of Purification. The Hopi name for the star Sirius is Blue Star Kachina. It will come when the Saquasohuh (Blue Star) Kachina dances in the plaza and removes its mask. According to Ancient Alien Theory, the Blue Kachinas are aliens. In Theosophy, it is believed the Seven Stars of the Pleiades transmit the spiritual energy of the Seven Rays from the Galactic Logos to the Seven Stars of the Great Bear, then to Sirius. From there is it sent via the Sun to the god of earth (Sanat Kumara)and finally through the seven Masters of the Seven Rays to the human race.

- **The Aztec:** in South America built pyramids and temples high in the mountains and they too point to the Pleiades group of stars. Some of the cut stone weight more than 100 tons. Scholars studying Aztec religion identified no less than 200 gods, divided into three groups, with each group supervising one aspect of the universe such as the heaven or the sky; the rain, fertility and agriculture; and finally the war and sacrifice. The Aztecs called the stars of Orion's Belt and sword the Fire Drill; their rising in the sky signaled the beginning of the New Fire ceremony, a ritual Aztecs performed to postpone the end of the world

- **The constellation Orion:** has their origin in Sumerian mythology, specifically in the myth of Gilgamesh.

Sumerians associated it with the story of their hero fighting the bull of heaven, represented by Taurus. They called Orion URU AN-NA, which means "the light of heaven." Their name for the constellation Taurus was GUD AN-NA, or "the bull of heaven." Orion is a well-known constellation in many cultures.

In Australia, the stars forming Orion's belt and sword are sometimes called the Pot or the Saucepan.

In South Africa, the three stars of Orion's Belt are known as Drie Konings (the three kings) or Drie Susters (the three sisters).

In Spain and Latin America, the stars are called Las Tres Marías, or The Three Marys.

- **Stone Hedge:** Archaeologists believe the stone monument was constructed anywhere from 3000 BC to 2000 BC as described in the chronology. The alignment also made it clear that whoever built Stonehenge had precise astronomical knowledge of the path of the sun and, must have known before construction began precisely where the sun rose at dawn on midsummer's morning. Stonehenge is not merely aligned with solar and lunar astronomical events, but can be used to predict other events such as eclipses. In other words, Stonehenge was more than a temple, it was an astronomical calculator.

- **The Antikythera Clock** : or Mechanism: remains a significant archaeological head-scratcher. Found in the sunken wreckage of a Greek cargo ship that is at least 2,000 years old, the circular bronze artifact contains a maze of interlocking gears and mysterious characters etched all over its exposed faces. Originally thought to be a kind of navigational astrolabe, archaeologists continue to uncover its uses and now know that it was at the very least, a highly intricate astronomical calendar. It is still the most sophisticated device ever found from that period, preceding the next appearance of similar devices by 1,000 years.

- **Crop Circles:** Twenty six countries reported approximately 10,000 crop circles in the last third of the 20th century; 90 percent of those were located in southern England. Many of the formations appearing in that area are positioned near ancient monuments, such as Stonehenge. In the 1960s, in Tully, Queensland, Australia and in Canada, there were many reports of UFO sightings and circular formations in swamp reeds and sugar cane fields. The most famous case is the 1966 Tully "saucer nest", when a farmer said he witnessed a saucer-shaped craft rise 30 or 40 feet (12 m) up from a swamp and then fly away, when he went to investigate. To date approximately 10,000 crop circles have been reported internationally.

- **Giants:** The Book of Giants, based on Enoch's scripts retells part of this story and elaborates on the exploits of the giants, especially the two children of Shemihaza, (Satin) Ohya and Hahya. Since no complete manuscript exists of Giants, its exact contents and their order remains a matter of guesswork. Most of the content of the present fragments concerns the giants' ominous dreams and Enoch's efforts to interpret them and to intercede with God on the giants' behalf. These giants were the offspring of the fallen angels (200 total) According to theosophists ape-like giants were the third root race who lived on the continent of Lemur. Theosophists also linked giants to the Atlantian's race. Occultists and Theosophists claim the stone structures were built by a race of giants. Madame Blavatsky claimed that the Easter Island stone structures were built by the fourth root race, a race of giants. It should also be noted that Giants were also involved in many other assisted building structures at Aztec, Mayan and Stone Hedge. Although never proven, the weight of the stones was massive in size.

- **Fallen Angels and their children:** Certain wise men of old wrote concerning them and say in their [sacred] books that angels came down from heaven and mingled with the daughters of Cain, who bare unto them these giants. But these [wise men] err in what they say. God forbid such a thing that angels who are spirits, should be found committing sin with human beings. And if such a thing were of the nature of angels, or Satan's, that fell, they would not leave one woman on earth, undefiled. But many men say, that angels came down from heaven and joined themselves to women and had children by them.

  This cannot be true. But they were children of Seth, who were of the children of Adam that dwelt on the mountain, high up while they preserved their virginity, their innocence and their glory like angels; and were then called 'angels of God.' But when they transgressed and mingled with the children of Cain and begat children, ill-informed men said that angels had come down from heaven and mingled with the daughters of men, who bear them giants.

- **The Temple of Ur in Iraq** The ziggurat was built by King Ur-Nammu who dedicated the great ziggurat of Ur in honor of Nanna/Sîn, in approximately the 21st century BC. The massive step pyramid measured 210 feet (64m) in length, 150 feet (46m) in width and over 100 feet (30m) in height. The height is speculative, as only the foundations of the Sumerian ziggurat have survived.

- The **Church of St. George** is one of eleven monolithic churches in Lalibela, A monolithic church or rock-hewn church is a church made from a single block of stone, believed to have been created in the 12th century. The most famous of them is the cross-shaped Church of St. George. Tradition credits its construction to King Lalibela, who was a devout Christian. The myth is the angels cut the rock at night and the local people cleaned up the debris during the day.

There are many less noted sites around the world. My point is; these structures and items cannot be explained away, yet they were here thousands of years before modern Technology was developed or heavy machinery. In fact, some of these stones could not be moved in place today with any of our modern machinery. What did the elder's know and who helped them build these sites? These sites were built by humans, or others, and they were certainly not built by God.

Of the lesser known structures around the world, I would point out one that is told by my son-in-law. His name is Toa Rodriguez (last name from the Spaniards) and he is from the smallest group of Islands in the middle of the Pacific Ocean.

- <u>**Federation of Micronesia**</u>: comprising dozens of small islands in the western Pacific Ocean. It is distinct from Melanesia to the south and Polynesia to the east. The Philippines lie to the west and Indonesia to the southwest. Only a few miles in size and most are inhabited today. Much of the area came under European domination quite early. In the early 17th century, Spain colonized Guam, the Northern Marianas and the Caroline Islands (what would later become the Federated States of Micronesia and Palau), creating the Spanish East Indies, which was governed from the Spanish Philippines. The Spanish government therefore decided to sell them to a new colonial power: Germany. Following Japan's defeat in the Second World War, its mandate became a United Nations Trusteeship, the Trust Territory of the Pacific Islands, ruled by the United States. Although not part of the US claimed islands like Samoa, it is considered a vital ally within the South Pacific. Christian missionaries in Micronesia have converted most of the people to either Catholicism or Protestant faiths. Traditional religion in Micronesian cultures involved belief in ghosts and ancestor worship. People also believed in spirits associated with specific places, objects and activities. Chants and offerings were directed to these patron spirits. Pohnpei is the largest and tallest islands.

Micronesia's best known archaeological site, Nan Madol-ancient city, the "Venice of the Pacific" is one of more than 100 sites of historical significance. According to legend, Nan Madol was constructed by twin sorcerers Olisihpa and Olosohpa from the mythical Western Katau, or Kanamwayso. The brothers arrived in a large canoe seeking a place to build an altar so that they could worship Nahnisohn Sahpw, the god of agriculture. After several false starts, the two brothers successfully built an altar off Temwen Island, where they performed their rituals. In legend, these brothers levitated the massive stones with the aid of a flying dragon. When Olisihpa died of old age, Olosohpa became the first Saudeleur. Olosohpa married a local woman and sired twelve generations. High walls surrounding tombs are located on Peinkitel, Karianand Lemenkou, but the crowning achievement is the royal mortuary islet of Nandauwas, where walls 18–25 feet

(5.5–7.6 m) high surround a central tomb enclosure within the main courtyard. Excavations show that the area may have been occupied as early as 200 BC. None of the proposed quarry sites exist in the area, meaning that the stones must have been transported to their current location. It has been suggested that they might have been floated to the site however; no one has successfully demonstrated or explained the process. Some modern Pohnpeians believe the stones were flown to the island by use of magic. Supposedly there was an escape tunnel beginning at the center of Nan Madol and boring down through the reef to exit into the ocean. Scuba divers continue to look for this "secret" route, but so far a complete tunnel has not been discovered. Keep in mind this megalithic structures contain stones or boulders weighing many tons each. My son-in-law thought the elders stories were crazy, or were they?

The point is somehow someone moved these large cut boulders up a mountain side and built this structure, and it was in the middle of nothing but ocean? Archeologists are baffled and still study it today.

CHAPTER 8

The Prophets of Old

There are many prophets as listed below, most of which were told by sacred books and some who envisioned in dreams. Only some saw God, Enoch was one. Note: his books were not included in the Bible, nor were 32 others. The Roman Catholic Church decided not to include them for unknown reasons at the time. Examples are the Book of Mary, Book of Judas and several others. They forced all books not included within the Bible to be destroyed by fire, some were buried for preservation, and the Dead Sea scrolls may have been a part of these forbidden scriptures.

LIST STARTING WITH THE BIBLE AND THE HEBREW BIBLE IN ALPHABETICAL ORDER:

Aaron (Exodus 7:1) Abel (Luke 11:50-51) Abraham (Genesis 20:7) Agabus (Acts 21:10) Agur (Book of Proverbs 30:1) Ahijah (1 Kings 11:29) Amos (Amos 7:8) Anna (Luke 2:36) Asaph (Matthew 13:35) Azariah (2 Chronicles 15:1) Barnabas (Acts 13:1) Daniel (Matthew 24:15) David (Hebrews 11:32) Deborah (Judges 4:4) Elijah (1 Kings 18:22) Elisha (1 Kings 19:16) Enoch (Jude 1:14) Ezekiel (Ezekiel 1:3) Gad (2 Samuel 24:11) Habakkuk (Habakkuk 1:1) Haggai (Haggai 1:1) Hosea (Hosea 1:1) Huldah (2Kings 22:14) Iddo (2 Chronicles 9:29) Isaiah (Isaiah 13:37)

Jacob (Genesis 28:11 - 16) Jehu (1 Kings 16:7) Jeremiah (Jeremiah 1:11) Jesus (God the Son and/or Son of God) (Matthew 13:57) Joel (Joel 1:1) John the Baptist (Luke 7:28) John of Patmos (Revelation 1:1) Jonah (Jonah 1:1) Joshua (Joshua 1:1) Judas Barsabbas (Acts 15:32) Lucius of Cyrene (Acts 13:1) Malachi (Malachi 1:1) Manahen (Acts 13:1) Micah (Micah 1:1) Micaiah (1 Kings 22:8) Miriam (Exodus 15:20) Moses (Deuteronomy 34:10) Nahum (Nahum 1:1) Nathan (2 Samuel 7:2) Noah (Genesis 7:1) Obadiah (Obadiah 1:1) Oded (2 Chronicles 15:3) Philip the Evangelist (Acts 8:26) Paul the Apostle (Acts of the Apostles 9:20) Samuel (1 Samuel 3:20) Shemaiah (1 Kings 12:22) Silas (Acts 15:32) Simeon Niger (Acts 13:1) The Two Witnesses of Revelation 11:3 Urijah (Jeremiah 26:20) Zechariah, son of Berechiah (Zechariah 1:1) Zechariah, son of Jehoiada (2 Chronicles 24:20)Zephaniah (Zephaniah 1:1)

PROPHETS OF ISLAM:

Adam, Idris (Enocha), Noah, Patriarch, Hud (Ebera), Saleh Abraham, Lot Ishmael, Isaac, Jacob, Joseph, Job, Shuayb (Jethroa), Moses, Leader Tawrat (Torah), Aaron, David, Solomon, Elijah, Elisha, Jonah, Dhul-Kifl (Ezekiela), Zechariah, John the Baptist , Jesus, Leader Injil (Gospel), Muhammad

Some had gone to Heaven and supposedly saw and spoke to God. Enoch was taken in the clouds and left earth somehow, and spoke to God, and came back to earth years later.

ENOCH

The brief account of Enoch in the book of Genesis says of him only that he "walked with God," Genesis 5 ends with the note that he "was not" and that "God took him." The question of what became of Enoch puzzled later generations. The 3rd century translators who produced the Greek Septuagint rendered the phrase "God took him". This recounts how Enoch is taken up to Heaven and is appointed guardian of all the celestial treasures, chief of the archangels and the immediate attendant on God's throne. He is subsequently taught all secrets and mysteries and, with all the angels at his back, fulfills of his own accord whatever comes out of the mouth of God, executing His decrees. Much esoteric literature like the 3rd Book of Enoch identifies Enoch as the angel, which communicates God's word. In consequence, Enoch was seen by this literature and the rabbinic kabbalah of Jewish mysticism, as having been the one which communicated God's revelation to Moses, in particular, the dictator of the Book of Jubilees. It is said that when Enoch returned to earth, he had knowledge superior to mortal man and his age was 365 years.

The remnants of several almost complete copies of The Book of Enoch in Aramaic were found among the Dead Sea Scrolls. Enoch lived before the Flood, during a time when the world, was immensely different. Human beings lived much longer, for one thing; Enoch's son Methuselah, for instance, attained the age of 969 years. Another difference was that angels and humans interacted freely, so freely, in fact, that some of the angels begot children with human females. This fact is neutrally reported in Genesis (6:1-4). According to The Book of Enoch, the mingling of angel and human was actually the idea of Shernihaza (AKA Satin) the leader of the evil angels, who lured 200 others to cohabit with women. The offspring of these unnatural unions were giants. Enoch's efforts to intercede with heaven for the fallen angels were unsuccessful (Enoch 6-16). For this reason, God determined to imprison the angels until the final judgment and to destroy the earth with a great flood.

MUHAMMAD

Muhammad was born in Mecca approximately 570 C.E. and was a member of the Quraysh tribe. As with Moses and Jesus, we know little about his childhood. His parents died when he was young, he was orphaned at an early age and brought up under the care of his uncle and he never learned to read or write. When he was about 40, Muhammad had an encounter with the angel Gabriel who revealed to him uncommon revelations. Three years after this event Muhammad started preaching these revelations publicly, proclaiming "God is One", that complete "surrender" to Him is the only way acceptable to God and that he himself was a prophet and messenger of God. In 632, a few months after returning to Medina from The Farewell Pilgrimage, Muhammad fell ill and died. By the time of his death, most of the Arabian Peninsula had converted to Islam and he had united Arabia into a single Muslim religious polity. The revelations (or *Ayah*, Signs [of God]")—which Muhammad reported receiving until his death form the verses of the Quran, regarded by Muslims as the "Word of God" and around which religion is Muslim based. Besides the Quran, Muhammad's life and traditions (*sunnah*) are also upheld by Muslims as sources of sharia law.

I find it fascinating that a man who could not read or write was able to bring a substantial religion, and an entire empire to revere him among all other Muslim prophets.

JESUS CHRIST (SON OF GOD)

The most influential figure of Christianity. Very little is known about his childhood other than the fact that his birth in mentioned in the Bible. Also referred to as Jesus of Nazareth, he is the central figure of Christianity, whom a majority of Christian denominations believe to be the divine Son of God. In Luke 1:31-38 Mary learns from the angel Gabriel that she will conceive and bear a child called Jesus through the action of the Holy Spirit. When Mary is due to give birth, she and Joseph travel from Nazareth to Joseph's ancestral home in Bethlehem to register in the census of Quirinius.

Following his betrothal to Mary, Joseph is troubled in Matthew 1:19–20 because Mary is pregnant, but in the first of Joseph's three dreams an angel assures him not be afraid, to take Mary as his wife because her child was conceived by the Holy Spirit.

In Luke 2:1–7 Mary gives birth to Jesus and, having found no place in the inn, places the newborn in a manger. An angel visits the shepherds and sends them to adore the child in Luke 2:22. After presenting Jesus at the Temple, Joseph and Mary return home to Nazareth.

Virtually all scholars of antiquity agree that Jesus existed. Most scholars agree that Jesus was a Jewish teacher from Galilee in Roman Judaea, was baptized by John the Baptist and was crucified in Jerusalem on the orders of the Roman Prefect, Pontius Pilate. Jesus was known as the Messiah, a charismatic healer, a sage and philosopher, or a social reformer who preached of the "Kingdom of God." As a means for personal and egalitarian social transformation Christians believe that Jesus was conceived by the Holy Spirit, born of a virgin, performed miracles, founded the Church, died sacrificially by crucifixion to achieve atonement, rose from the dead and ascended into heaven, from which he will return.

The majority of Christians worship Jesus as the incarnation of God the Son and the Second Person of the Holy Trinity. Jesus is considered one of God's foremost prophets. In Islam, Jesus is a bringer of scripture and the product of a virgin birth, but not the victim of crucifixion. Judaism rejects the belief that Jesus was the awaited Messiah, arguing that he did not fulfill the Messianic prophecies in the scripture. Jews almost never refers to Jesus as the Messiah. The words of Jesus with John the Baptist stating in John 3:34: "he whom God hath sent speaketh the words of God" and Jesus stating in John 7:16: "My teaching is not mine, but his that sent me" and again re-asserting that in John 14:10: "the words that I say unto you I speak not from myself: but the Father abiding in me doeth his works". With absolute certainty, God is the spirit within the body of Jesus Christ as the above statement implies.

Some believe the lost 18 years, as a time when Jesus travels to the centers of wisdom in India, Tibet & Western India, Persia, Assyria, Greece and Egypt. In each of these capital cities, he is educated, tested and teaches as a religious leaders. Jesus inevitably proves that he is 'God's chosen One' (the Christ) in these locales and brings back this multi-cultural wisdom and confidence to Galilee & Judea. Jesus puts on the role of The Christ, but is not automatically Christ by nature. By making himself, through desire, effort, ability and prayer, a fit vessel, Jesus enabled The Christ to dwell within him. Christ is therefore used as a term for the seemingly perfect human being that Jesus exemplified, a human being that has been "Christened" (anointed) and therefore made holy.

Jesus came to earth to show the way back to God via his lifestyle and teachings. He is the example we must model our own lives after, if we seek the highest dimensional level.

Reincarnation exists and karma ("You reap what you sow") is the explanation for various beliefs in many religions. In Matthew 11:27 Jesus claims divine knowledge, stating: "No one knows the Son except the Father, and no one knows the Father except the Son", asserting the mutual knowledge he has with the Father. Jesus' parables are seemingly simple and memorable stories often with imagery, and each conveys a teaching which usually relates the physical world to the spiritual world. Jesus asked his disciples; "But who do you say that I am?" Simon Peter answers him; "You are the Christ, the Son of the living God." In Matthew 16:17 Jesus blesses Peter for his answer and states: "flesh and blood hath not revealed it unto thee, but my Father who is in heaven." In blessing Peter, Jesus not only accepts the titles Christ and Son of God which Peter attributes to him, but declares the proclamation a divine revelation by stating that his Father in Heaven had revealed it to Peter. Jesus takes Peter and two other apostles with him and goes up to a mountain, which is not named. Once on the mountain, Matthew (17:2) states that Jesus "was transfigured before them; his face shining as the sun and his garments became white as the light. A bright cloud appears around them and a voice from the cloud states: "This is my beloved Son, with whom I am well pleased; listen to him "The Transfiguration not only supports the identity of Jesus as the Son of God (as in his Baptism), but the statement "listen to him", identifies him as the messenger and mouth-piece of God.

Notice that Jesus never saw God but he was the son of God and his teachings were of love and kindness to all. No one knows how he performed the miracles he did like raising the dead and healing the blind, among many others, and we will never know. The strong belief in Christianity is; you can only get to heaven through Jesus Christ, whereas other religions do not share the same teachings or beliefs. The Christian religion has the most followers, close to three billion, slightly less than half the world population. There are many branches of the Catholic religion such as Presbyterian, Lutheran, Orthodox, Seventh Adventist and Baptist among many others who follow the same Catholic beliefs with more or less emphasis on Jesus Christ and his teachings.

No one knows how he performed the miracles as stated, but we must remember, he was doing something miraculous, some two thousand years ago, under Roman oppression and rule. Of all the named prophets Jesus was the only person to perform miracles, including raising the dead, as well as himself. Crucifixion was the most common form of punishment in Roman times, cheap publicity for all to witness, and highly visible to thousands. It is said that Spartacus's army when captured, lined the trail all the way back to Rome, thousands hung on a cross to die. If done today and made public, the world would scream in outrage. Yes, the Romans were merciless and so were their successors. There are hundreds of books about Christ, and other prophets that are available everywhere and short of his miracles, he was a preacher, a messenger of God, like some of those mentioned above. The purpose of this book is not to point out any one person and it is included here for the sole purpose of religious beliefs and its followers. We all, with the exception of atheist, believe there is a higher being that will save mankind in some way, or another, in our hour of need. With the majority being Christians, theirs is Jesus Christ.

Today, there are those who claim to be prophets and claim to predict the future. There is one that stands out in modern times. His name was Edgar Cayce and he was called the sleeping prophet. His work and predictions are still being studied and discovered to by many groups of professionals around the world. Some of his prophecies included healings among other amazing abilities.

EDGAR CAYCE

Was an American psychic who possessed the ability to answer questions on subjects such as healing and wars, and even had visions of the world ending. He also gave a reading about Atlantis while in a hypnotic trance. Cayce founded a nonprofit organization, the Association for Research and Enlightenment. Though Cayce himself was a devout member of the Disciples of Christ and lived before the emergence of the New Age Movement, some believe he was actually the founder of the movement and influenced its teachings.

Cayce became a celebrity toward the end of his life and he believed the publicity given to his prophecies overshadowed the more prominent parts of his work, such as healing the sick and studying religion. Skeptics challenged Cayce's alleged psychic abilities and traditional Christians also question his unorthodox answers on religious matters such as reincarnation and the Akashic records. When the questioner asks where Edgar Cayce received his information, the answer would be, "We have explained before that the intelligent infinity is brought into intelligent energy from eighth density or octave." The term used for this is the "Akashic Record" or the "Hall of Records". Edgar used this gateway to view the present. However, others accepted his abilities as "God-given". Cayce described his own ailment from a first person plural point of view "we" instead of the singular "I". In subsequent readings, he would generally start off with "We have the body". Reports of Cayce's work appeared in the newspapers, which inspired many postal inquiries. Cayce was able to work just as effectively using a letter from the individual as with having the person present. Given the person's name and location, he said he could diagnose the physical and mental conditions and provide a remedy. Cayce soon became famous and people from around the world sought his advice through correspondence. Because of this, Cayce questioned his stenographer about what he said in his trance state and remained unconvinced. Cayce's methods involved lying down and entering into a sleep state, usually at the request of a subject who was seeking help with health or other personal problems (subjects were not usually present). The subject's questions would then be given to Cayce and Cayce would proceed with a reading.

Reincarnation was a popular subject of the day but not an accepted part of Christian doctrine. At first these readings dealt primarily with the physical health of the individual; later readings on past lives, business advice, dream interpretation and mental or spiritual health were also given. When out of the trance he entered, Cayce said he generally did not remember what he had said during the reading. The unconscious mind, according to Cayce, has access to information that the conscious mind does not—a common assumption about hypnosis in Cayce's time. Other abilities that have been attributed to Cayce include astral projection, prophesying, medium, viewing the Akashic Records or "Book of Life" and seeing auras. Cayce said he became interested in learning more about these subjects after he was informed about the content of his readings, which he reported that he never actually heard himself. As a humble individual full of self-doubts, Cayce never profited from his mystic gift. He read the Bible every day, taught Sunday school and helped others only when asked. Many did ask and over the years he produced readings that diagnosed health problems, prescribed dietary regimens, dealt with psychic disorders and predicted future events such as wars, earthquakes and changes in governments. He spoke moreover of reincarnations, the early history of Israel and the lost civilization of Atlantis. Enough of his diagnoses and predictions proved true to silence many skeptics and to develop a wide following. Cayce also predicted that records were made by the Atlantis civilization and were stored in three different locations around the world. One of which, is under the left paw of the Egyptian Sphinx. Ground penetrating studies have proved there is some sort of hollow cavity exactly where Cayce said it would be. For obvious reasons, if they are found, it would not be made public, as it would literally change the religious concept of Genesis or prove it to be correct. The other two are located somewhere in a tunnel system in South America and in the ocean by the Bahamas. To date, none have been made public. His namesake lives on in Virginia under the name Association for Research and Enlightenment.

CHAPTER 9

Understanding the Human Soul & Spirit

Accordingly, the Hebrew word nephesh, although translated as "soul" in some older English Bibles, actually has a meaning closer to "living being". According to Genesis 2:7 God did not make a body and put a soul into it like a letter into an envelope of dust; rather he formed man's body from the dust, then, by breathing divine breath into it, he made the body of dust live, i.e. the dust did not embody a soul, but it became a soul—a whole creature.

Adam become Man after (nshamah) the breath of God changed Adam into nephesh (man). This process is made clearer in John 3:6 in this way: "That which is born of the Spirit is spirit" and is confirmed in Luke 3:38 "Adam, which was the son of God" and finally in more detail in Hebrews 12:9, where God is the "Father of our spirit". In the Gospel of Matthew, Jesus asked his followers "For what is a man profited if he shall gain the whole world and lose his own soul?" (Matthew 16:26a) He also taught his followers to "fear not them which kill the body, but are not able to kill the soul: but rather fear him which is able to destroy both soul and body in hell." (Matthew 10:28)

The **soul**, in many mythological, religious, philosophical and psychological traditions, is the incorporeal and in many conceptions, immortal essence of a person, living thing, or object. According to some religions (including the Abrahamic religions in most of their forms), souls or at least immortal souls capable of union with the divine belong only to human beings. For example, the Catholic theologian Thomas Aquinas attributed "soul" to all organisms but taught that only human souls are immortal. It could refer to a ghost or spirit of the dead in Homer and to a more philosophical notion of an immortal and immaterial essence left over at death. Authorized King James Version "and fear not them which kill the body, but are not able to kill the soul: but rather fear him which is able to destroy both soul and body in hell." Although the terms soul and spirit are sometimes used interchangeably, soul may denote a worldlier and less transcendent aspect of a person. According to psychologist James Hillman, soul has an affinity for negative thoughts and images, whereas spirit seeks to rise above the entanglements of life and death.

The words soul and psyche can also be treated synonymously, although psyche has more physical connotations, whereas the soul is connected more closely to spirituality and religion.

The Ancient Greeks used the same word for 'alive' as for 'en-souled', indicating that the earliest surviving western philosophical view believed that the soul was that which gave the body life. The soul was considered the incorporeal or spiritual 'breath'. The soul sleeps while the limbs are active, but when one is sleeping, the soul is active and reveals itself in ones memory as dreams. Every individual dreams when they are sleeping, some do not remember any of their dreams, while others remember everything. We have all experienced what is called vivid dreams at some time in our life. These dreams are the unconscious mind being controlled by the souls data bank of information and interrupting it into a dream which in some cases seems so real, a person feels he or she is a part of it. Many cultures use meditation to obtain a higher vibration or frequency to enter into this dream like state, such as monks, physics, mediums, prophets and many other names, in an effort to either read a person, or gain knowledge of some event which may happens based on certain conditions.

SOCRATES AND PLATO

Plato, drawing on the words of his teacher Socrates, considered the soul the essence of a person, being that which decides how we behave. He considered this essence to be an incorporeal, eternal occupant of our being. As bodies die, the soul is continually reborn in subsequent bodies. The Platonic soul comprises three parts:

1. The logos, or logistician (mind, or reason)

2. The Thymus, (emotion, or spiritedness, or masculine)

3. The Eros, (appetitive, or desire, or feminine)

4. Each of these has a function in a balanced, level and peaceful soul.

Aristotle defined the soul or psyche as the first actuality of a naturally organized body but argued against its having a separate existence from the physical body. In Aristotle's view, the primary activity of a living thing constitutes its soul; for example, the soul of an eye, if it were an independent organism, would be seeing its purpose or final cause. Aristotle identified three hierarchical levels of living things. Aristotle concludes that the human active intellect is immortal. Perhaps, this is why studies have shown that when people are put in a hypnotic state, their soul, or spirit recounts past lives with detail of that time? Meaning the soul, or spirit of a person takes all the information of the brain it was once in and carries it with it from body to body through rebirth.

THOMAS AQUINAS

Concerning the human soul, his theory required that, since the knower becomes what he knows, the soul was certainly not Corporeal, the soul had an operation which did not rely on a bodily organ and therefore the soul could subsist without the body. Furthermore, since the rational soul of human beings was a subsistent form and not something made up of matter and form, it could not be destroyed in any natural process.

I believe, the more a young child learns from his or her surrounding, the more its brain is filled with material knowledge and the soul resides more into a dormant state but is still there absorbing the knowledge of that individual person's life. Something like learning and experiencing what it is to be that particular person with all his or hers life experiences, good or bad. Something many may not know, the word "psychology" literally means "study of the soul". Although the words soul and spirit are often viewed as synonyms, spirit is associated with afterlife, cosmic issues, idealistic values, hopes and universal truths, while Soul is associated with "in the thick of things" in the repressed, in the shadow, in the messes of life, in illness and in pain and confusion of love. No one is truly sure if both are separate or the same? In Christianity, it is called the spirit, meaning the essence, (energy) whereas the soul is the learning experience repository of knowledge within one's life, the memory of that individual.

Examples: he is a pathetic soul or poor soul and may the spirit be with you, or his spirit is now in heaven.

I personally think they are linked together with the soul as the memory and the spirit as the essence (electrical energy) that goes to another dimension after death of the human body. The soul is that which makes meaning possible, [deepens] events into experiences, is communicated in love and has a religious concern, as well as a significant relation with learning and death. The advances that have been made in science are steadily uncovering the validity of the concept of an independent soul mind and spirit. Ghosts are merely the essence, or energy of the soul and spirit choosing to stay within the realm of earth. To complete an unfinished task while they were alive, or a myriad of other reasons science is not sure of or understands. Some do not know they are (body) dead and others simply may be lost between dimensional levels.

Different religious beliefs of a person's soul and spirit include;

Egyptian religion, an individual was believed to be made up of various elements, some physical and some spiritual.

Similar ideas are found in ancient **Assyrian and Babylonian** religion.

The Baha'i Faith affirms that "the soul is a sign of God, a heavenly gem. Baha'u'llahs stated that the soul not only continues to live after the physical death of the human body, but is, in fact, immortal. Heaven can be seen partly as the soul's state of nearness to God; and hell as a state of remoteness from God. Each state follows as a natural consequence of individual efforts, or the lack thereof, to develop spiritually. Baha'u'llah taught that individuals have no existence prior to their life here on earth and the soul's evolution is always towards God and away from the material world.

Brahma Kumasi's, souls, are believed to be an infinitesimal point of spiritual light residing in the forehead of the bodies they occupy. Every soul has three separate faculties which are inherent in all human beings irrespective of place of birth. Just as electrical energy produces warmth, sound or light depending on the device through which it passes, similarly, the energy of consciousness functions through three different but closely connected faculties, referred to respectively by the terms mind, intellect and personality.

Buddhism teaches that all things are in a constant state of flux: all is changing and no permanent state exists by itself. To them, the word "soul" simply refers to an incorporeal component in living things that can continue after death. Buddhism does not deny the existence of the soul. Various schools of Buddhism have differing ideas about what continues after death.

Christians understand the soul as an ontological reality distinct from, yet integrally connected with the body. Its characteristics are described in moral, spiritual and philosophical terms. According to a common Christian eschatology, when people die, their souls will be judged by God and determined to spend an eternity in Heaven or in Hell. Some Christians believe that if one has not repented of one's sins and trusted in Jesus Christ as Lord and Savior, one will go to Hell and suffer eternal damnation or eternal separation from God.

There is also a belief that babies (including the unborn) and those with cognitive or mental impairments who have died will be received into Heaven on the basis of God's grace. Among Christians, there is uncertainty regarding whether human embryos have souls and at what point between conception and birth the fetus acquires a soul and consciousness. This uncertainty is the general reasoning behind many Christians' belief that abortion should not be legal. Bible scholars point out how spirit and soul are used interchangeably in many biblical passages. The soul, therefore, is not only logically distinct from any particular human body with which it is associated; it is also what a person "is".

Catechism of the Catholic Church defines the soul as "the innermost aspect of humans that which is of greatest value in them, that by which they are most especially in God's image. The soul signifies the *spiritual principle* in man. All souls living and the dead will be judged by Jesus Christ when he comes back to earth.

Eastern Orthodox and Oriental Orthodox views are somewhat similar, in essence, to Roman Catholic views although different in specifics. Orthodox Christians believe that after death, the soul is judged individually by God and then sent to either Abraham's Bosom (temporary paradise) or Hades/Hell.

Protestants generally believe in the soul's existence, but fall into two principal camps about what this means in terms of an afterlife. Some, following Calvin, believe in the immortality of the soul and conscious existence after death, while others, following Luther, believe in the mortality of the soul and unconscious "sleep" until the resurrection of the dead.

Christadelphians believe that we are all created out of the dust of the earth and became living souls once we received the breath of life based on the Genesis 2 account of humanity's creation. Adam was said to have become a living soul. His body did not contain a soul; rather his body (made from dust) plus the breath of life together were called a soul, in other words a living being.

Seventh-day Adventists believe that the main definition of the term "Soul" is a combination of spirit (breath of life) and body, disagreeing with the view that the soul has a consciousness or sentient existence of its own. They affirm this through Genesis 2:7 "and (God) breathed into his nostrils the breath of life and man became a living soul.

Jehovah's Witnesses take the Hebrew word *nephesh*, which is commonly translated as "soul", to be a person, an animal, or the life that a person or an animal enjoys. They believe that the Hebrew word *ruach* (Greek *pneuma*), which is commonly translated as "spirit" but literally means "wind", refers to the life force or the power that animates living things

Latter-day Saints (Mormons) believe that the spirit and body together constitute the Soul of Man (Mankind). "The spirit and the body are the soul of man" They believe that the soul is the union of a domain of 'Elemental Intelligence coeternal with God, a portion of God's spirit which gives life and a temporal body, which is formed by physical conception on earth. After death, the spirit continues to live and progress in the Spirit world until the resurrection.

In Hinduism For the soul, there is neither birth nor death at any time. He has not come into being, does not come into being and will not come into being. He is unborn, eternal, ever – existing and primeval. He is not slain when the body is slain." In Hinduism, the Sanskrit word most closely corresponding to the soul is "Aatma", which can mean soul or even God. It is seen as the portion of Brahman within us. Hinduism contains many variant beliefs on the origin, purpose and fate of the soul.

Islam teaches the soul is immortal and eternal. What a person does is certainly recorded and will be judged at the utterly court of the God.

In modern Judaism the soul is believed to be given by God to a person by his/her first breath as mentioned in Genesis, "and the LORD God formed man [of] the dust of the ground and breathed into his nostrils the breath of life; and man became a living being." (Genesis 2:7). From this statement, the rabbinical interpretation is often that human embryos do not have souls, though the orthodox often oppose abortion as a form of birth control. Judaism relates the quality of one's soul to one's performance of mitzvot and reaching higher levels of understanding and thus closeness to God. Though Jewish theology does not agree on the nature of an afterlife, the soul is said to "return to God" after death.

Other religious beliefs because the soul is said to be transcendent of the material existence and is said to have (potentially) eternal life, the death of the soul is likewise said to be an eternal death. Thus, in the concept of divine judgment, God is commonly said to have options with regard to the dispensation of souls, ranging from Heaven (i.e.

Angels) to hell (i.e. Demons), with various concepts in between. Typically both Heaven and hell are said to be eternal.

While others believe higher than the soul is the spirit, which is considered to be the real self; the source of everything we call "good—happiness, wisdom, love, compassion, harmony, peace, etc. While the spirit is eternal and incorruptible, the soul is not. The soul acts as a link between the material body and the spiritual self and therefore shares some characteristics of both.

The soul can be attracted either towards the spiritual or towards the material realm, being thus the "battlefield" of good and evil. It is only when the soul is attracted towards the spiritual and merges with the Self that it becomes eternal and divine. One with the Universal God.

The point is, 90 percent of religions believe there is a soul as well as a spirit. Soul and spirit are real and not a part of man's two dimensional world, it comes from God and is from a higher dimensional level. There are many reasons we as humans cannot see it, feel it, or understand it. We grow up in a material world, and the older a child gets the less connected it is to his or her soul and spirit. Another reason is the body is within a certain plain or dimension. I think of it as a different frequency. Also if one ponders the thought that it would be great if we were able to know who we were in a prior life or lives, we would be filled with constant bombardment of information which has nothing to do with our present life. It would be like trying to listen to dozens of radio stations at the same time. It would eventually drive one crazy. This is the sole reason the soul does not make it possible for one to know of their past lives.

Here is a perfect example of what I mean;

Radio and television waves (frequencies) along with many others are always in the air. If you turn on your radio and tune into a certain station, you hear what that station is playing, but you do not hear the thousands of other stations playing at the same time even though they are there. The same principles apply to Wi-Fi and Light waves. Fiber optics transfer information @ light speed. Some people can tune into certain frequencies when they claim they speak to the dead or spirits.

A young lady who is known as Theresa Caputo (AKA, The Long Island Medium,) which is broadcasted on the TLC channel, can tune into dimensional frequencies. She knows personal information about the people she reads that no one could possibly know except the person being read. She only asks for the person's first name and that is it, she connects with their deceased relationships they had in their life. In reality, she is constantly bombarded with souls trying to connect with her. Like Edgar Cayce, she can tune into the souls frequency. Of course, my question would be; how does the spirit, or soul show up from nowhere for that specific persons reading? Is the soul or spirit of the deceased, always following that person, or can it be called at will? The truth is, I do not know how, but Theresa does connect them somehow, someway. It may be the Akashic record spoken of by Edgar Casey and others. It is understood that the Akashic records hold all the information from the beginning of time into the future. A universal super computer made of the memory of souls. The recorded record of everything. This would also explain the statement in the Bible; God knows everything that has ever happened. Other mediums do the same, however they are not as well-known as Theresa Caputo.

<u>We are essentially spiritual beings having a human experience on Earth.</u> Although we might initially say that we "have" a soul, it is actually more accurate to say that we are a soul who "has" a body with personality, and this self-centered personality is our instrument of expression in the world around us. Until our personality is more purified and invokes the soul's help, it tries to run the show and often creates a mess.

In ancient Greece, the temple of the Oracle at Delphi proclaimed, "Man, know thyself and thou wilt know the universe and the gods. Today, modern science is beginning to prove the existence of the soul and its survival after the death of the body. To experience the soul, is to experience a deep sense of oneness with all that is.

Inner work and practice can help us build what's called the Rainbow Bridge (Eastern teachings) between our personality and soul. We can focus on thinking positively as an energy follow, understanding and looking for the good, the beautiful and the true in everything. Look into the essence of things, not just their outer form. In realizing, we are in essence the soul, the Divine light within, our purpose and work becomes clearer. To shine our souls light into the world and to relieve suffering, darkness and ignorance. By radiating the light of love and purpose, we help create a new heaven on earth. After all, we are all one with the universal energy of God. My message to mankind is straightforward "when pure unconditional love overcomes the love of power, we humans will be able to live in harmony with everything and anything".

CHAPTER 10

The Puzzle Come's Together

We as humans, think we have come a long way in time. The real fact is, we are but a millisecond of time as it relates to our existence on earth. Yes, we have come a long way from caves and sticks, but most of our technology has happened in the last 100 years compared to thousands of years mankind has been on this planet, that is a blink of time. If we continue to progress as fast as we have recently, we too could fly to other solar systems and be seen as gods to those inhabitants on another planet. The fact is, we are still playing in our own cosmic backyard and close to the back door at that. Yes, we have sent machines to mars this year and we have no idea what we will find. Imagine if we could go to other stars systems, what would we find? Are we the only humans in the entire universe, most certainly not! Let's play a numbers game for a moment. Let's say there are one million planets we know of and just one is close to earthlike? Would life form on it, over millions of years? Probably yes! Now times the possible planets that may produce life forms when you increase the amount of planets by two trillion, the possibilities are in the tens of thousands now. The only problem I see is, traveling between these planets. For us, it is light years to the nearest star. If we could travel at the speed of light, we could reach all the planets in our solar system within days. Is it possible for planets out there with intelligent life forms millions of years older than mankind to have the technology to travel on light beams itself? Or perhaps they can create worn holes within space as predicted by Albert Einstein? Einstein proved in his theory, it is possible for worm holes and time travel to exist. Our civilization would need another few hundred years of research and development just to develop a propulsion system for such a journey. Science is inventing new technology every week it seems, so it may be possible someday. I think the visionaries of our time were Carl Sagan, astronomer, and Gene Roddenberry creator of Star Trek.

"Who are we? We find that we live on an insignificant planet of a humdrum star lost in a galaxy tucked away in some forgotten corner of a universe in which there are far more galaxies than people".

CARL SAGAN

"Reality is incredibly larger, infinitely more exciting, than the flesh and blood vehicle we travel in here. If you read science fiction, the more you read it the more you realize that you and the universe are part of the same thing. Science knows still practically nothing about the real nature of matter, energy, dimension, or time; and even less about those remarkable things called life and thought. But whatever the meaning and purpose of this universe, you are a legitimate part of it. And since you are part of the all that is part of its purpose, there is more to you than just this brief speck of existence. You are just a visitor here in this time and this place, a traveler through it."

GENE RODDENBERRY

The meaning of life is a philosophical question concerning the significance of life or existence in general. It can also be expressed in different forms, such as "Why are we here?", "What is life all about?" and "What is the purpose of my existence?" It has been the subject of much philosophical, scientific and theological speculation throughout history. There have been a large number of proposed answers to these questions from many different cultural and ideological backgrounds.

The meaning of life is therefore, a religious conceptions of existence based on the belief of God, social ties, consciousness, happiness and many other issues, such as symbolic meaning, ontology, value, purpose, ethics, good and evil, free will, the existence of a or multiple Gods, conceptions of whom God is, the soul, spirit and the afterlife.

All of creation and all of existence are itself a part of God and we as humanity are unaware of our own inherent Godliness and are grappling to come to terms with it. The standing view in Hasidism currently is, that there is nothing in existence outside of God - all being is within God and yet all of existence cannot contain him. Regarding this, Solomon stated while dedicating the Temple of God, "But will God in truth dwell with mankind on the earth? Behold the heaven and the heaven of heavens cannot contain you".

We need only look at what was here before us to understand the wonders of the universe, let alone the wonders here on earth. There are signs everywhere showing that someone or something created mankind, built or were involved with structures of megalithic proportions and weight, with precision far beyond capabilities of primitive man. With all our knowledge and technology, we cannot give a definitive answer to any of these wonders which still stand today and may be here long after we are gone. Will we ever find the secrets of old? If we did, would we use them for good or evil? Will proof of the Atlantis records ever be found and showed? Will we ever know the truth of God and gods?

Julius Robert Oppenheimer, theoretical physicist and professor of physics known as the father of the atomic bomb remarked later that it brought to mind words from the Bhagavad Gita; "Now, I am become Death, the destroyer of worlds."

In the beginning of this book, I had questions. I still have questions and perhaps even more than before. To me life is an ever learning experience filling us with new ideas and information on a daily basis. The more we learn the more we understand our true past. Our soul sucks up knowledge like a sponge within our brain. It stores it and carries it upon a person's death. I believe our soul is the memory bank part of us and the spirit is the spark (energy) that keeps the body alive. They are intertwined as one, but separate within our bodies. Soul being the computer and spirit being our life force energy, which allows our heart and brain to function. Both in perfect harmony with each other, both leaving the body at death to a higher level. If not satisfied it returns in the form of reincarnation or rebirth to learn and experience human life again.

The debate concerning the existence of God is one of the oldest and most discussed in human history. One problem posed by the question of the existence of God is that traditional beliefs usually ascribe to God's various supernatural powers. Supernatural beings may be able to conceal and reveal themselves for their own purposes. In addition, according to concepts of God, he is not part of the natural order, but the ultimate creator of universal nature and of the scientific laws. Since God (of the kind to which the argument relates) is neither an entity in the universe nor a mathematical object. The fact that there is no conclusive scientific proof of his existence, or non-existence of God, demonstrates that the existence of God is not a scientific question but a religious belief.

Christianity and Judaism assert that God intervened in key specific moments in history, especially at the Exodus and the giving of the Ten Commandments in front of all the tribes of Israel, positing an argument from empirical evidence stemming from the sheer number of witnesses, thus demonstrating his existence. He also led the way through the use of magical powers possessed within the Ark and a flying object which the Israelites followed by day and night.

For the argument of the Resurrection of Jesus, This asserts that there is sufficient historical evidence for Jesus's resurrection to support his claim to be the son of God and indicates God's existence. This is one of several arguments known as the Christological argument.

Islam asserts that the revelation of its holy book, the Qur'an, vindicates its divine authorship and thus the existence of God.

The Church of Jesus Christ of Latter-day Saints, also known as **Mormonism**, similarly asserts that the miraculous appearance of God, Jesus Christ and angels to Joseph Smith and others and subsequent finding and translation of the Book of Mormon establishes the existence of God. The whole Latter Day Saint movement makes the same claim for example Community of Christ, Church of Christ (Temple Lot), Church of Jesus Christ, Church of Jesus Christ of Latter Day Saints, Church of Jesus Christ. They similarly asserts that the finding and translation of the Plates of Laban, also known as the Brass Plates, into the Book of the Law of the Lord

Most schools of Hindu philosophy accept the existence of a creator God (Brahma), while some do not. The school of Vedanta argues that one of the proofs of the existence of God is the law of karma.

Another class of philosophers asserts that the proofs for the existence of God present a fairly large probability though not absolute certainty. A number of obscure points, they say, always remain; an act of faith is required to dismiss these difficulties.

An argument for God is often made from an unlikely complete life reversal in lifestyle by an individual towards God based on near death experience or intervention by God or his angels.

When a person's understanding ponders over the existence of God it encounters nothing but contradictions; the impulses of people's hearts, however, are of more value than the understanding and thus proclaim clearly the truths of natural religion, namely, the existence of God and the immortality of the soul and spirit.

Modernist Christianity also denies the demonstrability of the existence of God. According to them, one can only know something of God by means of the vital immanence, that is, under favorable circumstances the need of the divine dormant in one's sub consciousness becomes conscious and arouses that religious feeling or experience in which God reveals himself.

Puzzle pieces:

- God saw there was Gold on earth; the Anunnaki saw there was gold on earth.

- God made man in southern Iraq; the Anunnaki made modern man in southern Iraq.

- God put the Garden of Eden by four rivers in southern Iraq; the Anunnaki made man in southern Iraq near four rivers.

- God called man Adam; the Anunnaki called man Adamu.

- The creation story (Genesis) is seven days; the epic of creation (Sumerian) is seven tablets.

- The Sumerians were the first civilization to invent writing, time, Calendar, astrology of our solar system including all the planets within it and the zodiac system. Not bad for a primitive race some six thousand years ago? They tell an incredible story on clay tablets about gods who were living among them at the time and in control of humans and demigods. They called their version of Adam creation, the creation of Atamu, which the Hebrew Bible translated to Adam. The Hebrew translation of Adamu is worker. They say that the Anunnaki (Elohim) made man in their image, through the medical manipulation of mixing DNA of the Anunnaki genes and homo erectus. Only in the past 15 years has today's scientists been able to clone vegetables, fruits and animals through genetic engineering.

• In speaking of genome engineering, we humans have 48 chromosomes. Well let me correct that, we actually have 46, chromosomes #2 and #3 are fused into one. They are not fused in monkeys, apes, or early man. That is what makes use different than ape-man. The fact that our 2nd and 3rd chromosomes are fused was not done by Mother Nature or Darwin's theory of evolution either. The most plausible explanation is that someone with a higher intelligence, be it God himself, or the Anunnaki created man. God never said he made man, he said "let us make man". We have no proof that God made man other than what was written in religious text. If one is to weigh the evidence, the Sumerian tablets give far more detailed information in the creation of man for a specific purpose and also would explain the experimental failures relating to various types of hominids and Greek mythology.

• The story of the Torah is from Hebrews' while in Babylon around 600 B.C.E. and the Sumerian epic which had been in existence and was written thousands of years earlier are almost exactly the same story, with minor changes over time. In addition to those facts, Babylon is where the Sumerian's lived. It is better known as Iraq today. Iraq is also said to be the cradle of civilization itself. Even though the most influential piece of the puzzle is provable fact based on the existence and Hebrew interpretation of stories passed down from generation to generation, I will leave judgment up to you as to whom you believe is true concerning creation of man. The Anunnaki may have even been the angels of God who made man.

- God is the Universal creator of everything. He is the universe itself. His essence is everywhere within the universe. His divine spark of life itself is in everything we see and touch. He is a vibration of music and sound itself. He is real, he is everywhere at the same time and therefore he is infinite. He is the maker of all that is. This should answer the question of who is God. The answer to what God is, he is the entity, essence, ether of the universe. He is not a person; although he can manifest his soul into a body (human) if he chooses, such as the case with Jesus Christ, however, he is within us, as we are part of him. We are made up of star dust, therefore, part of the universe itself. As to where God is, he is everywhere at the same time, he is the energy of the ever growing universe itself and still expanding. The akashic records are a part of him and we are a part of the akashic records connected via our soul.

- God breathe life into Adam which made Adam alive with a soul.

- Jesus Christ spoke many times of a man's soul and how it lives on after death.

- We on the other hand are merely the vessel in which his essence, soul and spirit resides. We have free will to do good or bad and God does not interfere with our choices. We, compared to the vastness of space and the unending universe are but a speck of sand on a tiny ball we call Earth. If we think for one minute we are alone in this universe, we are truly fools. God made everything and if he chooses to create within the universe, it is his to decide. As the Catholic Church stated, "we cannot put limits on God and his divine decisions".

- A Ziggurat is a temple tower of the Babylonians or Assyrians era, consisting of a lofty pyramidal structure, built in successive stages and a shrine at the top called also zikkurat. All Ziggurats resemble a three stage rocket in its design, which were and still are a house of worship and still built and used for the same purpose today.

I am sure we most likely were visited by a superior race of beings in the past based on the structures and writings which stood the test of time and remain today. Those which humans called gods of their time and depicted them with wings to represent flight. We have a different vocabulary and understanding from the days of old and if you or I saw something from the far future what would we call it, or explain it to be? There is an enormous amount of objects, structures, writings and information here on earth that we do not understand and cannot discard it as fairy tales, nor do we even understand how they came to be built. Using primitive tools so many years ago would result in primitive workmanship and we do not see that at all. Cut stones weighing hundreds of tons being moved up mountainsides. It would be a massive undertaking to duplicate it today with all our knowledge and machinery and yet we are to believe primitive man accomplished all this?

I am absolutely convinced someone had to be here helping and showing those primitive humans how. Too many unanswered questions around the world and our brightest minds are scratching their heads in awe. Most say 'It is impossible without help from superior knowledge, humans could not have done this alone". Many civilizations have perished before us with their knowledge and many will come after us with different superior knowledge. The age of the record player is long gone and 80 percent of kids today do not even know what a record player was, we live in an ever changing time and tomorrow will be smarter than today.

The Old Testament part of the Bible stands for itself and the religious beliefs of many, but I personally think it may be a different God it speaks of as described in the Bible. That does not change my faith in its writings, it allows me to see it in a different prospective than most.

The New Testament is absolute in its words from Jesus Christ. He is and will always be the essence, soul and spirit of the one true Universal God. His kindness, compassion, unselfish love for mankind and teachings were all about his God. He told us, "In my father's house, there are many mansions", if he is referring to the universe, than he is right, as there are more stars and planets than there are people on earth. God made many things within our universe and this may be only one of many universes. Who are we to say, we are alone in the universe? God could have, and most likely did make many forms of life in his infinite universe. We may never know.

CHAPTER 11

Life is a Mystery

For most of us, life is mundane and we go through it trying to survive and make ends meet. Some Choose to end it quickly while others rob and steal for survival. Others are victims, survivors, leaders and followers. But all of us pray when we are deeply troubled and need help. For me, I was never afraid of death, only how I died. When I was about eight years old, I was taken to the hospital for what later turned out to be blood poisoning and when I was old enough, around twelve, my mother told me that while in the hospital I had died after a routine spinal tap She was never told how long I was gone, only that my heart stopped and the doctor was able to bring me back to life. I remember that after leaving the hospital, I started having strange dreams, and was not sure what they meant. My mother later told me that I started asking about angels, God and family that had died. It was around the same time; my mother asked me to become an altar boy for the church, and introduced me to the priest in charge at Our Lady of Loreto Church in Brooklyn N.Y. My mother thought I would become a priest because of my death experience and constant questions about religion. Kind of odd, as my father worked for one of the five families at the time, and was not an attendee of the church however; I did not know that until I was in my teens. I was able to do mass in Latin after several months of training. For me, it was comfortable being inside the church with all the statues and Jesus on the cross, I felt like I had a connection with them even though they were not real. When I was around twelve, my mother sat me down and told me the story of what happened at the hospital that day and it hit me with fear and at the same time made sense as my dreams were still happening and becoming more intense for me to comprehend. Now I knew what the dreams meant and it became clear that they were a part of my dying experience. No one knows how long I was gone except the doctors and they never told my family.

My dreams always started out the same way, at least three times a week and lasted for almost three years. To this day, I am not sure if the dream was a byproduct of my dying, or if when I died I went somewhere and saw something. I was in the process of blood transfusion and heavily sedated at the time. I can only declare, when I died something must have happened to me and became a constant dream afterwards.

I remember seeing people I did not know and they were crowding around me and a man took my hand and walked me away from the others to a grassy hill, and there we sat and talked. He told me that I would have to go back because my mother had lost a son who was born before me and she could not live knowing she lost another child. I remember asking him who those people were and this person explained that they were family who had missed me and were waiting for the rest of us to come home. I did not understand what he meant by home? He told me that home was in heaven where God lived with his children, it was far away yet very close and this confused me. I remember asking him if this meant I would not be able to see my mother again and he laughed saying, "You can stay for a few moments, but your mother is waiting for you," and I would not be able to stay long. I asked him if he was coming with me and he held my hand and asked me to say how much he loved my mother and he would be there to help her when she was ready. I was not sure what that meant, but I do remember him telling me it was time to go back. I was sad and happy both at the same time, knowing I would be seeing my mother and give her this message, and sad that I was leaving this gentle man whom I did not know, but had a connection to in a strange kind of way. I asked him his name as we walked back to the bottom of the hill, he kissed me on the head and said his name was John. He put his hands behind me and gently pushed me into some type of spinning tunnel which looked like a neon slide. It was but a second when I was back in my hospital bed where I saw my mother and father crying by my bedside. I do remember telling her many days later about the man I meet and what he said to me. When she asked me if I knew his name, I told her and she gasped for breath and starting walking fast to retrieve a picture of which she showed me, "Is this the person you saw" she asked crying, I told her he was younger but, yes he looked like the man I saw. It was my grandfather, whom I had never seen, as he died at the age of 43 and I was born years later with his name sake.

My mother died when she was sixty four from lung cancer, and the strange thing is, her last words to her younger sister was " I am tired and want to go home", the fact is, she was already home in a hospital bed which was setup in the living room. Her sister told her it was OK to go home and my mother closed her eyes and died moments later. Was her soul speaking out loud for the first time? What was strange to me was the saying of "home". No one knows what she meant by using the word home? I remembered, my grandfather telling me that heaven was home for those who passed and here, at my mother's death bed, she wanted to go home. She was thirteen months to the day her sister was born and died thirteen months to the day her sister died of lung cancer also. My father died one and half years later of a broken heart.

I am sure my near death experience was the catalyst for my curiosity into religious matter as it was a strong part of my past. Many parts of life are a mystery to us because we do not understand the nature of different dimensions, or where they come from, or how they happen. From time in history to present day, we still hear of miracles, ufo's, new finds, strange objects and more, and no one has the absolute answers to an afterlife or what a soul is. As much technology as we have, no one is able to completely answer some of the complex questions about life and what has been left for us to wonder about, such as the megalithic structures around the world. Science has been studying these structures for answers, and has been doing so for many years without ever getting any closer to how it was done. Doctors and the medical field still do not understand the entire brain or what 95% of our DNA actually does in our body. Granted, they are all making strides in the understanding and breaking ground on new finds every week in the medical field.

Dolly the sheep was the first cloned sheep we know of; however scientists around the world have been manipulating genes for the last twenty years. The fact is, if science is capable of manipulating genes and creating new species, is it possible that thousands of years ago, we too were engineered by a superior race of non-human beings? Even if it was God of the Bible who created man, it is still a fact that he engineered us. The major problem with this theory is, dust is mostly carbon with trace elements of minerals, certainly not what humans are completely made of and therefore highly improbable. The more likely scenario might be, the stories from the Sumerian clay tablets explaining the manipulation of hominids already here on earth, making us the final product, homo sapiens, after unknown numbers of mishaps which may be part of Greek, Egyptian, Sumerian and many others mythology, of depictions of animal like beings. From Anubis to Zeus, from the griffin to the Pegasus, either our ancestors had imaginary minds, or they drew on something that they saw as real and recorded such in scriptures and drawings.

It is much easier to dismiss what we do not understand, but we humans are inquisitive and need answers to our questions. Perhaps this is why many of the ancient stories are still alive and researched by various groups. We obviously have not been content with the answers from professionals and the mystery only gets deeper the more we investigate.

In one hundred, years, we have gone from horse and buggy, to jets and computers. Technology has, and continues to leap forward every year. We have gone from little towns where everyone knew each other and helped their neighbors, to texting on a phone, socializing online, watching reality TV and becoming desensitized to violence and death through Video games and violent movies as well as television shows. Technology has allowed the prosperous countries to become lazy and stupid by performing technical task for us. Our children leave schools with less knowledge than 30 years ago. The use of computers to correct spell, communicate for us, socialize with friends and family, calculate numbers and even give us directions while driving have allowed humans no need learn for ourselves, how to make a change at a store without the use of electronics, no need to read a map or learn correct spelling and more.

In many ways, technology has hurt humans by allowing computers to do things for us and making us dumber over time and more dependent on technology. Think I'm wrong, try getting change from a young store clerk without using a register and see what happens. If the power goes off on earth, many would be lost and not know what to do with their time. All systems would be in complete shut down as they are reliant on electronics. We live in a world where computers perform most of our daily interactions with the outside world. For some secret societies, that is exactly what they intended. It is easier to control dependent people, than educated people.

The Bible is one of the oldest books still in publication today and I do not challenge its origin or scripture, I do however question the information pertaining to some parts, such as the coincidence, that there are stories very similar and the fact that they may have been interdicted for a specific reason or by mistake. The miracles stated within the Bible are perhaps the most compelling proof that somehow, someone or something is able to intervene on behalf of mankind for reasons we do not yet understand. The fact that miracles still happen today is evident that we have not been forgotten over time and are in some unknown way connected to a superior being for purposes we do not comprehend.

By making small changes in our lives, it can bring us closer to the Universal God. Do some charity work in your neighborhood, plant flowers in your yard, get back to nature, meditate ten minutes a day to relieve stress and heal yourself. Try to connect with your inner self, give to others rather than receive, pray and most of all, look at the world around you with unconditional love and compassion for those less fortunate.

In closing

It has been said that "money is the root of all evil" well that is not true. The fact is "Greed and selfishness are the root of all evil", Money is a tool of which to change ones greed"

"Our true history may be decidedly different from what we have been taught throughout the ages, whether this information has been withheld on purpose or our true identities have just been hidden for some purpose; it is our responsibility to rediscover who we are and where we are going".

Yes there is a God and he is not human, although he can manifest his soul and spirit into a human at any time in their life, as he must have with various prophets like Jesus, Mohamed and others. He is as the Bible said, everywhere at the same time, see's everything, knows everything and is a part of everything including us humans. If one considers the Anunnaki who were worshiped by the Sumerians did, as a God, than it would be easier to understand the Genesis theory in the Bible and why it was so prevalent within the ancient god stories and is still being understood today.

"May your soul seek true wisdom, happiness and unselfish love to others, and your spirit be forever connected to all of Gods energy and wonder around you".

Visit my website for more updates or contact me @ www.godandthegods.com

Recommended Reading

Complete Collection Set Books 1-7 (The Earth Chronicles, The 12th Planet, The Stairway to Heaven, The Wars of Gods and Men, The Lost Realms, When Time Began, The Cosmic Code, The End of Days) [Paperback] Zecharia Sitchin

Lost Technologies of Ancient Egypt: Advanced Engineering in the Temples of the Pharaohs by Christopher Dunn (Jun 24, 2010)

The Giza Power Plant : Technologies of Ancient Egypt, Lost Technologies of Ancient Egypt: Advanced Engineering in the Temples of the Pharaohs.3.The Giza Power Plant : Technologies of Ancient Egypt by Christopher Dunn (Aug 1, 1998)

Technology of the Gods: The Incredible Sciences of the Ancients by David Hatcher Childress (May 2000)

Ancient Egypt 39,000 BCE: The History, Technology and Philosophy of Civilization X by Edward F. Malkowski (May 14, 2010)

The Ancient Alien Question: A New Inquiry into the Existence, Evidence and Influence of Ancient Visitors by Philip Coppens and Erich von Daniken (Nov 15, 2011)

The Sumerians: Their History, Culture and Character Samuel Noah Kramer February 15, 1971

Corrections and or acknowledgments will be added as needed for any credits due to others provided such proof is accurate and true.

References

Wikipedia.org A free online encyclopedia (501c) supported by donations

King James Bible

Jewish Torah

Muslim Qur'an

The Washington Post Jun 15, 2011 01:25

Zecharia Sitchn author, writer, scholar http://www.sitchin.com/

http://www.lbl.gov/Science-Articles/Archive/Genomics-Neanderthal.html

University of Chicago report http://www.hhmi.org/news/lahn3.html

http://news.bbc.co.u/2/hi/americas/7973274.stm

http://mathildasweirdworldweblog.wordpress.com/category/uncategorized/

http://reinep.wordpress.com/2011/09/16/update-alien-annunaki-grave-yard-found-in-africa/

http://en.wikipedia.org/wiki/Giants

http://www.genome.gov/

http://www.veteranstoday.com/2012/09/17/ufo-war-chinese-and-us-navy-off-san-francisco/

http://www.liveleak.com/view?i=133_1348110214

http://en.wikipedia.org/wiki/Plagues_of_Egypt

http://www.atlantis.to/Jon Peniel.

www.reversespins.com/patton.html

http://www.catholicnewsagency.com/news/

www.bibliotecapleyades.net/sumer_anunnaki/esp_sumer_annunaki01.htm

www.youtube.com/watch?v=PZgUSUjzaYA

www.ancientx.com/

www.archaeology.org/1005/etc/conversation.html

www.edgarcayce.org/

www.are.org/

http://en.wikipedia.org/wiki/FOXP2

http://www.hhmi.org/news/lahn3.html

http://en.wikipedia.org/wiki/Donald_Johanson

http://en.wikipedia.org/wiki/Liger

http://en.wikipedia.org/wiki/Giant_(mythology)

http://en.wikipedia.org/wiki/Genesis_creation_narrative

http://en.wikipedia.org/wiki/Nobility#.22Blue.22_blood

http://en.wikipedia.org/wiki/Royal_blood

http://en.wikipedia.org/wiki/Extraterrestrial_life

http://en.wikipedia.org/wiki/First_Council_of_Nicaea

http://en.wikipedia.org/wiki/Asteroid_belt

http://www.metaresearch.org/solar%20system/cydonia/proof_files/proof.asp

http://en.wikipedia.org/wiki/Cuneiform

http://www.brlsi.org/events-proceedings/proceedings/25023

http://en.wikipedia.org/wiki/Hamlet's_Mill

http://en.wikipedia.org/wiki/Flinders_Petrie

http://en.wikipedia.org/wiki/Mithraic_mysteries

http://en.wikipedia.org/wiki/Hall_of_Records

http://en.wikipedia.org/wiki/reincarnation

http://en.wikipedia.org/wiki/Soul

http://en.wikipedia.org/wiki/Spirit

http://en.wikipedia.org/wiki/Mythology

http://en.wikipedia.org/wiki/Jesus

http://en.wikipedia.org/wiki/Star

http://en.wikipedia.org/wiki/Heaven

http://www.frozenark.org/news

04140578-00923003